Bid Management

A Guide to the RFP Process

Jeff Nguyen

Contents

Introduction

Responding to complex requests for proposals (RFPs) represents a defining challenge for vendors targeting new business. Submitting a winning bid takes insight into client needs, marketplace dynamics, and core principles of positioning amid competition.

This guide outlines key context on RFP processes and developing sharper proposals. We'll explore bid team roles, competitive factors, response best practices, and philosophy around continuous improvement. The goal is clearly framing the RFP landscape for strategic positioning.

The Bid Team Mission

At its core, a high-performance bidding team must consistently win their "fair share" of business in hypercompetitive markets to ensure organizational stability. This requires understanding customer requirements and challenges at a visceral level.

Bid teams target opportunities aligning well to their capabilities. They avoid situations obviously favoring niche competitors. Through this selectivity, teams enhance win predictability on bids pursued.

When targeting appropriate RFPs, mastery involves fully satisfying needs through competitive pricing combined with lucid value showcasing. Any deficiencies undermine positioning vulnerable to exploitation by insightful competitors. Excellence consists of articulating technical synergy and vision while easing concerns through demonstrated dependability.

Only through balance of these factors - intimate customer understanding, strategic selection, comprehensive optimization, and credibility signaling - can bid teams fulfill their essence of protecting corporate continuity in challenging landscapes through their "fair share" won consistently through quality, not quantity, of submissions mounted.

Sizing Up the Competition

Securing decisive victories requires surpassing not just the average bid, but a select group of particularly astute competitors who consistently submit the most compelling proposals.

To maintain an edge, teams must objectively evaluate their capabilities relative to these formidable opponents through meticulous market intelligence collection and performance analysis. Only a few bidders in any given pursuit typically showcase a level of sophistication combining advancements in offerings with deep understanding of client priorities and pain points. It is precisely by benchmarking continuously against these high-achieving organizations that bid squads stay focused on constantly refining and strengthening weaknesses to the standard essential for success. Moreover, the bar rises quickly as innovative practices and strategies proliferate across the industry.

Thriving in this progressively intensifying environment demands teams persistently elevate every aspect of their competitive positioning over time, whether through more imaginative solutions development, streamlined production methods, polished proposal composition, or optimized cost structures. Complacency is not an option, as those who rest on past accomplishments are certain to lose ground. Only through a dedication to ongoing enhancement and an keen awareness of rivals' evolving strengths can a proposal team reliably surpass top contenders and ensure winning margins endure.

Crafting Winning Responses

Comprehensively knowing a client's key concerns and evaluation approach determines RFP destiny. Submissions lacking resonance with assessor priorities face early dismissal, regardless of supplier talents.

This customer focus starts in advance of the final bid through engagement supplying strategic perspective. Squads also study past purchasing rationales for recurring themes.

Victorious proposals express suitability purposefully at each stage, from polished composition signaling professional capability to solution designs showcasing flawless implementation. Rather than alone hyping supplier achievements, responses frame worth methodically in relation to target client imperatives.

By carefully aligning the total response - from initial interest generation through final mark - teams showcase thorough focus on what elevates the client, now what elevates the brand. Proposals translate capabilities into language evaluator biases comprehend as precisely fulfilling their situation rather than broadly promoting skills. Customer fixation proves the differentiator between also-rans and leaders in any competitive landscape.

Sharpening the Approach

Above all, elite proposal teams nurture mindsets of relentless betterment regardless of present triumphs or setbacks. They methodically evaluate past performance seeking transferable insights for forthcoming solicitations.

Post-bid client debriefs surface perspectives facilitating organizational evolution. Analyses of such feedback weigh self-assurance and disappointment to distill realities from errant impressions.

Willingness to channel learnings into refinement readies teams to prevail gradually. While competitors rest on past wins, enhanced squads raise capabilities meeting evolving needs. Experience fosters intuition, yet only through open-minded review and incorporating third-party perspectives do teams avoid stale practices exceeding their usefulness.

Success stems less from single victories than constantly honing weaknesses revealed through measured retrospection. Astute suppliers invest in ongoing development, appreciating short-term outcomes alone fail to dictate future preparedness. Perpetual sharpening through disciplined self-assessment and stakeholder transparency secures market leadership enduring beyond momentary triumphs fleeting as circumstances.

The bidding journey demands commitment but brings huge rewards.

Chapter One

Understanding RFPs

A request for proposal (RFP) is a business document that announces and provides details about a project, solicits bids for its completion, and outlines the requirements that the winning bid must meet. Understanding the different aspects of RFPs is key for professionals looking to win new business. This article will explain what an RFP is, why they are used, their components, and best practices for crafting an effective proposal.

A RFP is a document issued by a business or organization that seeks to outsource a project or purchase a product or service. It contains all the information vendors need to understand the needs, expectations, and parameters of the work so they can submit accurate proposals and pricing. Common reasons organizations issue RFPs include lacking internal resources or expertise to handle projects themselves or wanting to leverage external solutions or ideas.

RFPs allow purchasers to provide details on their needs and solicit solutions or approaches from multiple vendor partners. They enable direct product/service and price comparisons across respondents. Overall, the RFP process aims to help purchasers clearly communicate needs and select the vendor best equipped to successfully deliver based on their methodology, experience, capabilities, and cost structure.

While specifics vary, RFPs generally include information like background on the issuing organization, a problem statement or needs summary, project goals/objectives, project scope and specifications, timelines, budget estimates, proposal instructions, and terms and conditions.

Some RFPs are highly detailed while others leave room for vendors to help shape solutions. Understanding all provided parameters is critical for developing compliant, competitive proposals. Vendors should analyze RFP content closely so they can ask clarifying questions, identify unstated needs, and put together the strongest response highlighting their differentiated value. We'll explore proposal best practices next.

The Purpose of RFPs

RFPs serve the dual purposes of defining project scopes and persuading vendors to want to work on those projects. Understanding why organizations issue RFPs in the first place can help professionals tailor stronger responses highlighting their unique value. This article explores the varied situations calling for RFPs, their intention to drive deals, parallels with project management methodologies, and how bid and project managers play different roles.

RFPs must both outline tangible objectives and convince respondents they want the business. The "define" aspect covers what the project entails and the expected costs or investment required. Details specifying deliverables, timelines, requirements, terms, and more allow bidders to accurately understand scopes.

The "persuade" dimension gives organizations issuing RFPs a chance to sell partners on the value of supporting their needs. They must compel respondents to bid by positioning the project as compelling and impactful. Highlighting prestige, partnership benefits, revenue opportunities, or other upsides can further entice responses. Overall, RFP creators must strike the right balance of defining parameters while persuading audiences to buy into the vision.

Why Issue RFPs? Seeking Deals Through Competition

Fundamentally, RFPs aim to drive deals and partnerships around business needs requiring external expertise or solutions. The competitive bidding process compels providers to put forth their best effort and pricing to win selection. Organizations issue RFPs when they cannot sufficiently address a project internally, want to leverage innovations from the open market, need to demonstrate due diligence around major spend decisions, or require comparability across vendor options before committing.

While RFPs imply major projects, even basic product quotations or service bids serve to outline offerings and convince customers. Details like service specifications, terms and conditions, and pricing still provide definition and persuasion albeit in simpler proposals. More complex RFPs around extensive IT implementations, long-term professional service contracts, infrastructure deployments, or other multifaceted projects take the dual purposes of definition and persuasion to another level.

Parallels to Project Management Principles

Interestingly, the sales journey instigated by RFP processes closely mirrors project management lifecycles. Planning proposals involves many of the same best practices around resource allocation, budgeting, scoping, scheduling, and delivery. Like technical project managers, bid managers must skillfully steer resources to deliver a quality outcome on time and on budget.

Yet while projects allow some fluidity between scope, budget, timeline, and quality, RFP responses fix most parameters. Their strict deadlines and specific demands limit negotiability. Additionally, success is not measured by coming in early or under budget. The sole focus is producing high-quality responses before the closing deadline to boost selection odds. This divergence shows bid and project management, while similar, require distinct expertise.

Understanding the unique intentions and constraints of RFP responses versus standard project plans can help professionals excel on both sides of the equation. Those looking to sharpen RFP practices specifically can apply project wisdom while also acknowledging key differences.

RFPs ultimately drive deals and partnerships critical for organizational success. Those who appreciate their varied applications, strategic role in buying processes, and parallels with project can master response techniques meeting both definition and persuasion needs.

Importance of RFPs in the Sales Process

Requests for proposals (RFPs) play an invaluable role across every major B2B sales cycle. understanding how to navigate RFPs can make or break deals worth millions in revenue. This piece explores why excelling at the RFP process must be a core sales capability and how to approach it for maximum success.

Significance for Driving Deals

RFPs signify serious purchasing intentions. Organizations issue them when committed to solving a business need requiring substantial budget and cross-departmental coordination. They indicate mature buying journeys ready for final vendor selections. Sales teams who view RFP invites as hard-won opportunities and not boilerplate obligations gain an edge.

Strong RFP responses underpin contracts with major customers. Decisions ultimately come down to who impresses on paper and in final selection pitches. Focused effort devoted to understanding RFP parameters, aligning solutions, detailing value, and quantifying capabilities pays dividends. The work leading up to contract negotiations depends heavily on RFP depth.

Partnership Potential

Earning business via RFP builds foundations for long-term relationships. Vendors should view selection as the beginning of maximizing customer value over years-long deployments together. Strong post-sales and account management depends on closely aligning to needs outlined in original RFP scoping. High performance strengthens bonds and referability.

Conversely, organizations issuing RFP value respondents exhibiting genuine commitment. Engaged, insightful proposals signal interested partners versus vendors chasing contracts. Asking thoughtful questions, identifying gaps proactively, and going above minimum requirements shows dedication coveted in major supplier relationships.

Required Expertise

As essential sales processes, RFP capabilities separate leading teams. Mastery requires attention to detail, coordination across functions, executive alignment on positioning, and tight orchestration. Bid managers must juggle many moving pieces from timely access to accurate pricing all while crafting compelling value narratives.

Investing in streamlined RFP operations, technology, and training elevates success rates in competitive review processes. Specialized skills in areas like terms and conditions navigation, integrations specification, security audit support, ROI modeling, and more provide edges. Expert proposal professionals assist overstretched sales teams struggling with RFP minutiae.

Mastering the complex interplay of logistics, positioning, relationships, and writing is no small feat. But those taking RFP capabilities seriously gain trust as partners and consistently win against rivals.

Process Advantages

RFP mechanics confer inherent benefits. Setting formal parameters ensures vendors solve the right business needs not tangential "nice-to-haves". It enables "apples to apples" comparisons across solutions on exact criteria. And structured selection procedures prevent decisions from becoming purely political or based on internal relationships.

On the provider side, RFPs allow asking clarifying questions essential for scoping accuracy. They ensure everyone competes on a level playing field with equal information. Review stages also grant opportunities to stand out from the pack by surpassing basics. For such a rigid process, RFPs enable significant creativity and relationship building around aligned solutions.

Flourishing within the RFP process proves mandatory for ambitious sales teams targeting seven and eight-figure deals with large customers. From shaping strategy to winning partnerships, executing proposals requires specialized expertise provided by the best bid management groups. Invest continually in the end-to-end RFP lifecycle to sustain competitive advantage.

How RFPs Differ from Other Sales Documents

From RFQs to RFIs and beyond, professionals regularly encounter various proposal-related acronyms. Understanding differences between requests for information (RFIs), requests for quotations (RFQs), and requests for proposals (RFPs) sharpens bid strategy. Despite their structured appearance, each sales document serves unique purposes requiring tailored approaches.

Request for Information (RFI)

RFIs represent preliminary explorations organizations undertake before committing to projects. They gather data around capabilities, methodologies, or feasibility to inform later decisions. RFIs involve no expectations of binding offers and minimal time investments for broad perspective gathering only.

Given their open-ended nature, responding to RFIs focuses on education. This presents excellent opportunities for shaping early thinking by showcasing expertise, sparking ideas, ou or flagging potential obstacles. Treat RFIs as relationship building and profile raising springboards for future sales conversations.

Resist proposing precise solutions too early unless RFIs show projects reaching advanced stages.

Request for Quotation (RFQ)

RFQs signify narrowed scopes requiring specific budgetary estimates. They provide detailed project parameters for vendors to offer binding quotations often spanning a few pages. RFQs represent serious buying intentions around relatively simple purchases with clear specifications.

Winning RFQ selection depends on accurate assessments of work required and providing the best rates. Avoid inflated estimates that fail to win on price or lowballing that ultimately erodes margins. Analyze RFQ fine print allowing revisions if early assumptions prove flawed. With RFQs, precision and restraint balance to optimize value.

Request for Proposal (RFP)

In contrast, RFPs detail complex projects with lengthy selection processes requiring extensive proposals spanning hundreds of pages. They demand investments of time and strategic resources equivalent to sales opportunities worth hundreds of thousands or millions.

RFP focuses expand far beyond quotations to position vendors based on comprehensive capabilities, integration capacities, experience, dedicated support models, roadmaps, and more. While RFQs zero in on project pricing, RFP success requires aligning wide-ranging methodologies and engagements across organizations. Investments in understanding RFP parameters and crafting solutions accordingly enable enterprise partnership wins.

Each sales document plays specific roles businesses can understand for smarter resource allocation and shaping advantage. Precisely matching levels of effort and messaging to RFI, RFQ, and RFP nuances accelerates revenue.

Chapter Two

The RFP Process

S uccessful organizations keep a pulse on upcoming RFPs long before they formally commence. Through established customer intimacy and market awareness, they gain insider word on emerging requirements and buyer priorities months in advance. This enables subtly influencing project scopes toward their strengths and expertise areas before RFP documents even published.

Well-connected teams access early intelligence by networking beyond immediate buyer contacts into wider stakeholder spheres. Developing relationships across legal, compliance, user and technical groups reveals crucial insights on future RFP direction. Sales and marketing players overly focused on individual champions miss key strategy inputs from broader organizational units.

Equipped with informed foresight into RFP themes, forward-thinking vendors direct customer mindshare toward favorable narratives aligning with advantages. For example, catching wind of a major technology overhaul RFP allows cloud-centric providers to position infrastructure modernization as a priority concern through thought leadership. This primes audiences to value specific messaging and capabilities later when RFPs launch.

Shaping stakeholder perspectives toward existing competencies early on makes eventual requirements seem tailored uniquely for your solutions versus competitors. Rivals must play catch up fitting square pegs into round holes as teams with advanced visibility push narratives underscoring strengths. This encapsulates sales wisdom - you close deals on your terms when possible.

Additionally, anticipating RFP subjects allows producing customized assets like case studies, architectures, metrics reports and more demonstrating expertise. Pre-compiled content carries more weight than hastily assembled bid collateral. And having in-house libraries prepared reduces chaotic scrambles covering RFP protocols from scratch during compressed response windows.

In the high-stakes RFP process, fortune favors the prepared. Major pursuits only come once in every few years amid lengthy enterprise sale journeys. Seizing fleeting competitive opportunities means stepping in with nurtured relationships, directed narratives, and readily proving credentials. No time or margin for catch up exists during tight RFP schedules. Getting a head start makes or breaks deals.

Requirement Issued

The RFP process formally kicks off when the buying organization publishes the request document outlining project parameters, expectations, timelines, and proposal instructions. This represents the start gun for vendors to begin developing responses aimed at winning selection. Carefully analyzing details within the RFP provides the foundation for shaping compliant, competitive proposals.

Opportunity Reviewed

Next, interested teams conduct initial opportunity reviews examining their fit, capabilities to address all requirements, appetite for investment relative to deal size, and probabilities of winning based on incumbent status or buyer relationships. Decision makers determine whether committing full resources makes strategic and financial sense given historical win rates and pursuit costs.

Resources Allocated and Planned

Upon greenlighting participation, vendors appoint "capture managers" to spearhead responses and assign cross-functional talent spanning technical, pricing, writing, and reviews. Planning which subject matter experts draft which sections prevents overlap or gaps while playing to individual strengths. Many moving parts require coordination.

First Draft

With teams and plans in motion, writing commences covering initial responses to all instructions, formatting, page limits, and areas specified per RFP requirements. This constitutes the foundational content conveying value, methodologies, experience, and pricing. Subsequent drafts refine messaging and details further.

Review

Cross-functional peer reviews ensure proposals effectively showcase capabilities aligned to buyer needs. Constructive feedback identifies gaps requiring additional evidence, clarification, persuasive messaging, visuals, proof points, etc. Reviews also confirm compliance in formatting, protocols, and included attachments.

Later Drafts and Reviews

Reviews generate successive draft iterations strengthening proposals through sharpened messaging, added specifics, edited clarity, and enhanced visuals. Subject matter experts must synthesize inputs balancing perspectives. Additional reviews follow each draft to maintain quality.

Sign Off

Final drafts undergo executive sign offs verifying alignment with strategic positioning, financial commitments, and accuracy. Formal approvals often require CEO or CFO review ensuring oversight on large competitive pursuits.

Production and Submission Accurate reproduction and timely submission stays vital as due dates approach. Teams carefully verify final formatted copies match final approved proposals before formally sending per delivery instructions. Digital and printed copies may both require submission. Missing deadlines instantly disqualifies otherwise strong proposals.

While written responses make up the core RFP activity, pricing, technical literature, demonstrations, security audits, references, and other elements require equal attention to complete packages. While requests for proposals can vary, time is always limited given the significant coordination required across teams. However, those who adequately prepare in advance by planning ahead can reduce unnecessary last-minute stresses and rushed work. Advanced planning helps ensure organized and efficient responses despite tight deadlines.

RFPs and Procurement Cycles

Understanding the cyclical lifecycle of requests for proposals (RFP) sharpens strategy for maximizing repeat business. Large organizations issue recurring RFPs around major budget items, usually on 12, 24, or 36-month horizons. Viewing engagement through a periodic lens uncovers retention and growth opportunities that may be hiding in plain sight for sales.

Planned Recompetes

In enterprise procurements for services, technology platforms, infrastructure projects and more, RFPs reissue on regular intervals per policy. For example, multi-year IT outsourcing contracts undergo mandatory rebids every 2-3 years. Facilities management, security services, digital agency partnerships follow similar cycles.

Purchasers managing eight and nine-figure relationships cannot continuously renew single vendors without opening refreshed competitions. RFP prohibitions on solesourcing over certain budget thresholds necessitate rebids despite satisfactory incumbent performance. Planning cycles account for these recompete RFPs.

Strategic Incumbency

In theory, incumbents hold inherent advantages from established scopes, data access, and customer intimacy. Yet without concerted efforts, familiarity breeds complacency not contract renewal. Overconfidence leaves door open for competitors.

Wise incumbents avoid this by working present contracts with future RFP cycles firmly in focus from the outset. This includes gathering feedback during deployments, identifying emerging needs, observing purchasing habits/policies and maintaining relationships beyond primary point of contact.

Most critically, they reaffirm commitments by delivering consistent excellence that compels partners to welcome re-signings. Avoiding major failures and anchoring partnership values sets the stage to contend reproposals. Embedding flexibility into original contracts also allows adjustments to meet evolving landscapes by renewal time.

Preparing Early Challenges

Contrarily, new challengers must properly size cyclical RFP windows into long term strategy. Pursuing organizations with 3+ year contracting horizons requires patience and sustained brand building before viable competition attempts.

Efforts initiate through progressive profiling activities across stakeholders, researching procurement histories, identifying upcoming projects by monitoring budgets. This girds competitive knowledge while nurturing influencer ties over years not months. Come RFP season, challengers leverage relationships and demonstrated capabilities to contend realistically from solid groundwork.

Whether current provider or outside disruptor, RFP history repeats for those taking the long view. Over multiyear journeys with major customers, organizations issue enough RFPs representing millions in recurring business to warrant such investments.

Beyond financial gains reaped in eventual contract wins or renewals, embedded positions deliver invaluable stability, referrals, prestige and RFP process mastery for application across broader pursuits. Harnessing repetitive RFPs unlocks exponential gains over the lifespans of long relationships, especially on bigger stages. All selling into major accounts unfolds through cycles beyond individual sales. RFPs epitomize these episodic journeys. Plotting work streams, partnerships and progress across these procuring patterns allows maximizing ROI over the long run.

Roles and Responsibilities of Stakeholders

Major RFP pursuits require extensive cross-departmental collaboration spanning numerous roles for seamless process execution and compelling final proposals. Understanding primary stakeholders, obligations, and subject matter expertise levels proves critical given intricate dependencies. This hinges on expertise, commitments and effective handoffs between numerous stakeholders. Well-integrated teams successfully balancing priorities amid the moving pieces gain a collaborative advantage.

Bid Manager

The bid manager, sometimes also called the capture manager, deal manager, or pursuit manager, leads RFP responses end-to-end, commanding resources and priorities while maintaining holistic oversight across workstreams. They manage schedules, budgets, cross-functional alignments toward qualitative proposals, drive executive reviews, and steer key strategic response decisions as the overarching authority.

The bid manager must also liaise closely with account managers to leverage existing customer intimacy for insights around evaluation committee priorities and implied needs. Beyond submission, they ensure proper handing over of pricing details and response specifics to delivery/implementation teams for consistency post-win.

Proposal Writers

Skilled proposal writers serve an invaluable role shaping documents that position vendors favorably while complying with requirements. They collaborate with SMEs to translate technical details and value propositions into persuasive content. Writers also maintain consistent voice and narrative flows customers can readily digest.

Strong grasp over qualifying criteria and reviewer types allows writers to emphasize connections between capabilities and desired evaluation areas. They further highlight strengths through clarity, compelling messaging, visual aids, and crisp formatting hitting all RFP specified guidelines. Editing inputs to retain coherence poses another key writing responsibility.

Pricing Leads

Pricing leads keep proposal costs aligned to budgets by coordinating centralized pricing teams and distributed unit financial planners. They compile inputs across project scopes, commercial constraints, terms and conditions, to binding integrated totals for senior approvals.

Pricing leads must command pricing methodologies and models to drive accuracy checking over intricate proposal calculations. Responsiveness to cost adjustments stemming from changing requirements or new information also falls under pricing lead oversight.

Subject Matter Experts (SMEs)

While numerous specialists operate in supporting roles, SMEs hold distinguished status, embedding critical technologies and domain expertise into responses. As foremost authorities over solutions intricacies, SMEs directly address technical RFP stipulations conveying innovation advantages and implementation capacities.

They further serve indispensable functions during Q&A sessions demonstrating fluency that inspires customer confidence in capabilities. SME influence permeates written content as well given dependencies on their insights explaining complex methodologies. Supplying clarity around technical specifics also falls to SMEs during proposal drafting as writers translate concepts into accessible depictions.

Reviewers

Reviewers scrutinize RFP responses to validate overall quality, completeness, persuasive appeal, clarity for customers, visual impact, and adherence to formal RFP requirements. Cross-functional peer reviews leverage multiple lens to improve proposals, including SME assessments confirming technical rigor and accuracy.

Reviewers also verify content maps comprehensively to evaluation criteria. This prevents gaps or imbalanced focus detracting from competitiveness. Review consolidation and dissent resolution represents another big responsibility to progress proposals positively between drafts toward coherence.

Common Pitfalls in Bid Management

Between tight timelines, intricate requirements, and cross-functional coordination, RFP responses sustain heavy lifting prone to missteps. Understanding frequent challenges encountered when orchestrating proposals sharpens mitigation tactics for smoother bid execution. Here, we examine typical pitfalls and best practices for evasion of each pitfall.

Disjointed Messaging

Inconsistencies plague responses stemming from isolated Planning becomes cohesion's enemy. Customers endure confusion facing unclear connections between high-level solutions, technical capabilities, financial impacts, and other key sections composed independently.

This fragmentation originates from siloed working - discrete parts written separately lose sight of the proposal's overarching story. Coordinated development from the project's inception supports a smooth storyline. Joint tools enabling real-time collaboration let the narrative flow naturally versus assembled piecemeal. Crafting a consistent message also requires workshops aligning contributors and style guidance maintaining a unified voice.

Central editors prove pivotal by preserving through-lines the customer can follow neatly. Their bird's-eye view catches disconnects others may miss immersed in details. Organized planning and cooperative authoring are the keys to presenting a clear and compelling customer journey.

Misinterpreting Requirements

Careful analysis and cross-checking helps ensure requirements are properly understood. With RFPs stretching to daunting lengths, it's easy for teams to misunderstand exact response instructions. As a result, they may neglect asked-for details or reuse outdated tactics no longer fitting the present scope.

To guard against misreads jeopardizing competitiveness, rigorous analytical processes are vital. Having bid managers lead collaborative walkthroughs protects consistent comprehension. Pre-planning workshops also forestall unfounded assumptions from contaminating the response as individual authors work from a unified framework. Cross-functional discussions dissect nuances confirming all parties interpret needs consistently.

Requirements analysis demands meticulousness given misaligned responses miss the target. Thorough processes jointly examining every stipulation from various angles arm teams to deliver proposals precisely tailored as clients require. This attention to accurate decoding gives proposals their best shot at advancing.

Undervaluing Compliance

Teams are often too excited to show what they can do. They forget to follow all the small requirements about formats, page limits, files types, and other rules. But not following directions is the same as not applying. The client may ultimately reject the proposal even if the ideas are good.

It's important to carefully check that the proposal fits all the rules. Reviewing the rules is a required step before submitting. Dedicated editors also carefully read the entire proposal against the rules to make sure nothing is missed. The fine print is just as important as the big ideas. Ignoring small details means the good ideas won't matter. Taking time to get the rules right is essential to moving the proposal to the next review stages.

Insufficient Review Cycles

It's common for teams to feel rushed when bids are due soon. They may not take enough time to have others read their work. But having only the primary team see drafts means mistakes can hide until it's too late.

Major problems, like forgetting price tables or inconsistent tone, may not appear until final checks. That causes panic close to the deadline. Last minute fixes feel messy and disorganized.

Requiring formal reviews at key points, such as outlines, early drafts, midway drafts and finals, helps find and fix issues gradually. Everyone sees each section develop step-by-step. Small mistakes don't pile up unseen until panic sets in.

Taking time for staged peer checking spreads out error-catching. It results in polished, coherent submissions without last minute hassles. A quality bid depends on steady, collaborative reviewing throughout the process.

In isolation, each misstep creates recoverable setbacks, but simultaneous over-sights stack these same deterrents against selection. Averting preventable errors through early mitigation tactics helps to sustain competitive RFP positioning.

Chapter Three

Managing Bids

S uccessfully responding to complex requests requires significant collaboration across departments involving document management, staffing planning, quality checking, capturing lessons, and other administrative areas. This
guide brings together best methods across all the internal processes that ensure
smooth proposal development for increased chances of winning.

By establishing strong basic systems that facilitate coordination, accuracy, uni-
formity and responsibility behind the scenes, sales groups can better concentrate
on creating compelling messages and demonstrating solutions. Well-organized
proposal management ultimately enables teams to consistently deliver high
quality responses efficiently. With proper internal governance, they can successfully replicate approaches for multiple opportunities.

Strategic Planning for RFP Responses

Successfully orchestrating multifaceted RFP responses amid intense pressures
requires structured planning and coordination across teams, timelines, and
workstream interdependencies. Here, we cover proven planning frameworks,
roles, and platforms streamlining coherent and compelling proposals.

Team Member Roles

Centralizing responsibility of assignments prevents duplicated efforts or gaps through clear delineations:

Writing Leads: Head writers spearhead foundational content and narrative development spanning executive summaries, project approach specifics, case study detailing, and core value proposition crafting based on intimate customer knowledge.

Editors: Editorial leads oversee maintaining consistent voice, style, format compliance, visual impact standards, and overall polish in collaboration with writers. They also manage final quality assurance reviews.

Bid Manager: The overarching program manager aligns teams, resources, abstract strategic imperatives from corporate directives into response priorities and designs guiding principles for cogent content.

Contributor Subject Matter Experts: Distributed SMEs feed vital expertise into relevant sections but require guidance translating technical depth into accessible depictions. Writers vet inputs accordingly.

Pricing Leads: Pricing analysts compile validated cost models, risk-adjusted margin projections based on terms and conditions, leveraging financial advisors.

Shared Platforms and Cadences

Digital workspace systems centralize distributed drafting, review tracking, and asset compilation in a common environment with access controls. Structured team spaces organize cross-functional proposals development workflows allowing real-time commenting and version control for streamlined collaboration at scale. Automated notifications signal review requests and approvals enabling easier traceability across stakeholders.

Platform analytics provide capture managers fuller oversight tracking progress percentages by section. This prevents lagging portions going unseen and stagnating overall timeliness.

Additionally, enforced regular sync rhythms through both centralized digital spaces and dedicated meetings cadence alignment. Bid kickoffs orient all players, while twice weekly reviews tackle high-level status updates, risks, decisions tracking, and mitigation brainstorming across department leads if needed.

Employ Proven Bid Techniques

Adapting reputable response templates, workflows, content frameworks, and analytical models refined across industry pursuits speeds aligned execution versus reinventing custom approaches. Training contributors on standard methodologies also raises capabilities through knowledge sharing.

Documented best practices from previous RFPs should be used to further govern bid activities for consistency. Templates facilitate rapid assembly of compliant responses while allowing customization for differentiation against competitors.

Guiding Principles

Proposal development principles codify priorities fostering consistency:

1. **Group insights over individual:** Feedback loops generate 360 perspectives benefiting proposals. Siloed standpoints invite blindspots. Collaboration rules.

2. **Framework before details:** Strategic narratives and value chain depictions guide granular capability inclusion so contributors plug into bigger pictures. Scattered tactical strengths dilute persuasion. Structure focuses relevance.

3. **Consistency across touchpoints:** Every RFP engagement surface – written content, verbal pitches, pre-recorded demos, live Q&As – drives alignments to customer priorities. Mixed messaging risks confusion.

4. **Balance brevity and depth:** Concise explanations demonstrating

comprehensiveness, supported by appendices showcasing further expertise. Noise hampers clarity.

5. **Preparedness over urgency:** Cross-team coordination prevents chaotic final stretches enabling smooth last mile executive reviews, formatting, and submission sign offs.

RFPs inherently require substantial effort due to their complex nature. However, a strong commitment to strategic planning of responses and collaboration between all stakeholders can significantly reduce disorganization. With expertise in managing well-structured processes, teams can better navigate challenges and more effectively achieve their goals even under pressure of tight deadlines and complex requirements. Advanced preparation and coordination are key to succeeding despite inherent difficulties.

Streamlining Proposal Development Through Document Controls

Large proposals spanning hundreds of pages with input from many people require structured systems to manage the document development process.

Proposal responses are document-centric. Seamless workflows between aligned versions, consolidated constructive feedback, definitive milestone drafts, and accessible archives accelerate collaboration and excellence. Taming logistical document challenges allows effort to focus on sharpening messaging and positioning instead.

Without tools to manage version flow, feedback consolidation, milestone draft archiving, and more, productive team collaboration stalls.

Version Tracking

Unorganized draft iterations confuse contributors when edits overlap or get misaligned. Team members may not know which version is definitive. Best practice naming conventions systematically classify draft versions by number and include metadata like author, date, and change summary.

For example, file names like v1_Initial Outline_GL_20230117 denote the first draft outline authored by Greg Lane on January 17, 2023. Tracking tables catalog all named drafts with metadata for quick reference on existing materials.

Number sequences also signal a single source of truth across editions. Teams can label subsequent drafts from reviewers v2, v3 and so on, with the highest sequence draft denoting the working authority copy.

Feedback and Markups Consolidation

Collaborative markups require policies so scattered inputs aggregate back into evolving drafts. Mandating highlights for additions and bubbles for critiques structures feedback for writer synthesis.

Likewise, embedded commentary tools create perceptible, actionable change logs. Requiring version notes explaining adjustments also improves context for evaluating revisions. Consider also adding a date and time to each comment for tracking.

Consolidating distributed remarks further eases reconciliation as drafts progress. Assigning editors to compile feedback matrices reconciling which changes got accepted, rejected, or need follow-up clarifies inconsistencies.

Archiving Milestone and Final Versions

At each major milestone - outline, initial draft, interim review, final pre-submission - master files preserve milestone states protected from subsequent tweaks. Like software golden builds, definitive drafts provide restoration points if quality checks catch downstream defects requiring reversion to known good states.

Archives should also retain legacy draft snapshots for future reference to recreate or avoid former directions based on past RFP outcomes. Analyzing dated versions grants rearview visibility to optimize future proposals based on lessons learned.

Optimizing RFP Resourcing

Major RFP pursuits require extensive resourcing across many departments to assemble robust responses. While significant investments are imperative, scaling bid investments proportionately to deal sizes and win probabilities determines positive ROI. Right-sizing resource allocations through selective criteria and centralized oversight is key to sustaining efficient results.

Cultivating Relevant Research

Abundant background inputs like analyst reports and news events exist publicly. But excessive context risks diluting persuasive messaging instead of sharpening insights.

Research efforts should isolate information specifically addressing buyer pain points, evaluative criteria, hot button issues, or competitor weaknesses that shape priorities. This refinement in your research targets signals directly relevant to the selection factors of the RFP issued instead of tangential noise.

Securing Committed Team Members

While some RFP requirements leverage dispersed subject matter experts (SMEs), named core staff securing firm time investments proves critical for informed perspectives. Stakeholder mapping visualizes needed talent by identifying topic adjacencies.

Relationship mapping then targets ideal SMEs based on customer contacts, past projects, and capability alignment. Direct outreach secures initial "quick win" confirmations before expansion. Leadership reinforcements ensure teams protect commitment levels despite other priorities.

Engage Cross-Functional Expertise

Tapping contributors across all pertinent capabilities, seeking alternate risk perspectives outside core teams, and engaging both senior executives and hands-on practitioners ensures responses speak authoritatively across the range of evaluator concerns. Assessing resource expertise against bid requirements further optimizes engagement.

Evaluating Expenses Against Potential Value

Meticulous effort-to-value tracking calculates proposal spend commensurate to prospective contract worth through modeling major cost drivers against win probabilities such as:

- Labor: time investments x hourly rates

- Research: market/competitive intelligence purchases

- Travel: live meetings incurring charges

- Production: printing, software licensing

Dividing aggregated expenses by win odds ratios determines reasonable upper spend thresholds before diminishing returns. Precedent analysis guides build-or-buy decisions on committing major investments against conservative expectations.

Oversight for Continuous Visibility

Estimating total resource needs helps executives approve new pursuits or adjust staffing. Continuous monitoring also allows real-time trajectory adjustments.

Centralized bid management systems consolidate timesheets, expenses and task completions compared to initial plans and budgets. Automatic notifications alert managers to potential cost overruns that could exceed guidelines. This oversight maintains alignment between investments and revenue expectations.

Careful selectivity, commitment tracking, cost-benefit modeling, and budget governance helps balance efficient resourcing with robust RFP responses to drive value. The right oversight and flexibility supports high performance against revenue targets.

Implementing Quality Control Procedures

Responding to RFPs necessitates robust quality control and administrative procedures. This is to validate completeness, ensure accuracy, evaluate from the client perspective, capture critical knowledge, and enable continuous improvement. Investing in these foundational areas allows sales operations to enhance consistency, replication, and optimization over recurring pursuits.

Verify Accuracy for Credibility

Thorough quality control builds credibility by validating all figures, data points, and messaging while meticulously proofreading to confirm accuracy and specifics. This attention to detail prevents avoidable errors that could undermine perceptions of competence, trustworthiness, or qualification.

Ensure Consistency for Professionalism

Cross-checking data, formatting, graphics, and other elements for consistency also enhances professionalism by coordinating a polished, aligned appearance across all collateral. Reviewing systematic quality scorecards on requirements conformance further objectifies this perspective.

Adopt Client Mindset for Relevance

Stepping into the client's shoes provides invaluable insight on how messaging and positioning resonates with their perspective. Assessing responses from the evaluator standpoint exposes assumptions requiring further validation. Role playing scoring scenarios tests persuasive impact more objectively than subjective internal reviews.

By prioritizing quality control and administrative procedures in responding to RFPs, sales operations enables higher quality, consistent, accountable, and optimized pursuit execution for improving win rates over time.

Administration of Bids

Responding to RFPs requires comprehensive administrative procedures for tracking tasks, archiving information, and assessing performance. Investing in these foundational areas allows sales operations to enhance accountability, consistency, and continuous improvement over recurring pursuits.

Capture Task Status for Accountability

Diligent tracking against RFP worksheets logs meetings, decisions, and accomplishment status across all workflow steps. Following standardized templates governs responsible task ownership for replying to buyer queries, gathering personnel approvals, completing subject matter reviews, and more with proper diligence.

Archive Institutional Knowledge for Replication

Centralized archives preserve response collateral, research library references, lessons learned assessments, and other documentation for easier replication in future pursuits. Cataloging this knowledge also promotes identifying best practices for continuous improvement rather than reinventing approaches from scratch.

Evaluate for Ongoing Optimization

Structured bid assessments analyze win/loss performance data, document trends across responses, and compile findings into shareable best practice guides. Root cause analyses on pricing, messaging, resource allocation also inform targeted improvement areas with the greatest ROI based on empirical evidence.

By prioritizing administrative procedures in responding to RFPs, sales operations enables higher accountability, consistency, and optimized pursuit execution for improving win rates over time. Robust administration is imperative for replicating success.

Final Thoughts on Managing Bids

Competitive RFP responses depend on the coordinated functioning of many interrelated internal processes. While compelling solutions may stand out publicly, strong foundations in areas like planning, document quality, efficient staffing, thorough quality reviews and robust administration ultimately determine how well execution is carried out.

Gaining expertise in these important organizational elements lets sales teams dedicate more effort to distinct marketing messages. Consistently using systems, guidelines and lessons learned helps institutionalize repeatable practices, continuously boosting win rates through standardized excellence over time. The right basic support infrastructure frees frontline staff to focus more strategically. It allows complex bids to be managed far more deliberately and impactfully.

Chapter Four

Deciding to Bid or Not Bid

C ontractors often talk about their success in terms of 'hit rates' – one in four, say, or one in three. The question is which one in four, which one in three? What you ought to be winning are the contracts that will do mostto help you achieve your marketing objectives, gain sustained income and add professional value to your services.

Completing a pre-qualification questionnaire and writing a tender can entail a substantial commitment of time, money and other resources that might well be spent more productively in other ways or on other possibilities. The decision to bid needs to be based on a realistic and carefully weighed assessment of the opportunity, its potential benefits and its costs.

Whether to bid on a contract depends on many factors including a company's finances, capabilities, staffing needs and technology. It also involves considering strategic plans, the type and size of work, client details, and any existing relationships.

If the initial decision is to bid, further evaluation of project details will be needed later. However, this first step focuses on high-level factors to judge the overall suitability rather than define the proposal contents. Financial situation, operational capacity, technical resources, strategic direction, professional requirements, scope, duration, client identity and status, and relationships all provide important context for weighing whether it makes sense to pursue the opportunity.

Factors Influencing the Competitive Situation

Assessing the chances of winning a contract requires understanding political factors like the customer's objectives and priorities. Similar to high-stakes poker, discerning clues about the buyer's motivations and competitors' strengths is crucial for strategizing effectively. Gathering additional insight into who else is bidding, their capabilities, and relationship with the client also provides valuable context when determining the best proposal approach. Careful consideration of these dynamics surrounding the competitive landscape and different stakeholders is foundational for positioning the bid for optimal chances of success.

Gauging Real Likelihood of Win

Before investing significant resources, determine whether the RFP represents a genuine award opportunity or merely an obligatory formality. Even officially open procurement situations may have underlying biases against change due to:

- Backroom Commitments to Incumbents: Longtime vendor relationships cultivate buyer inertia or seal handshake agreements obstructing fair consideration.

- Influential Internal Lobbying: Entrenched executive sponsors, tie-ins with preferred IT systems, or change-averse end user groups lobby against perceived disruption.

- Compliance Drivers: Some RFPs follow required competition procedures without serious intent shift vendors.

Uncover true prospects through probing satisfaction levels, stakeholder alignments, differentiators, and priorities to expose hidden agendas or predetermined outcomes. Buy signals like pressing buyer pain points, transparent scoring methods, access to economic decision makers and vetting your qualifications indicate viable chances worth pursuing.

Researching and Benchmarking the Competitor Field

Entering RFP situations without grasp of the competitor landscape invites nasty surprises when appraising formidable entrenched incumbents or niche players. Investing in thorough rival research prevents squandered efforts better redirected toward more favorable situations.

Profile strengths and weaknesses across capability factors like geographic presence, remedy offerings, delivery track records, pricing models and cultural fit. Maintain an evergreen perspective on threats by tracking indicators over time including win/loss rates, shifting positioning, new hires, capability investments and more.

Understanding Internal Client Relationships

Given equal capabilities otherwise, strong executive relationships confer powerful advantages securing mindshare, gathering intelligence, and building trust. Map relationships at the senior levels to reveal potential barriers or leverage points influencing selection decisions. Targeted networking with pivotal technical evaluators or end user groups helps offset disadvantages.

Weighing intelligence across these core areas provides the indicators needed to judge situational favorability and determine appropriate pursuit resourcing levels aligned with win prospects.

Strategic Bid Positioning for Long-Term Goals

RFPs demand substantial investments, so pursuits target opportunities accelerating strategic growth priorities beyond individual deal value. Carefully evaluating procurement alignments with target markets and assessing how prescribed terms and conditions could enable or obstruct wider progress ensures positions advance sustainable returns over one-off gains.

Evaluating Market Development Potential

Progressing top-line revenue growth and market share means selecting positions forging fresh inroads and differentiation, not just protecting existing domains. Prioritize bids cultivating new niche sectors or buyer categories over merely solidifying current strongholds vulnerable to shifting preferences or declining budgets over time.

Target underserved market adjacencies allowing specialty diversification at reasonable capability investment levels and acceptable risks to core business. Avoid harmful brand associations from overextending into areas conflicting with current perceived strengths or partner ecosystems.

Vet opportunities against total addressable market models, capability roadmaps, portfolio synergies and forward indicators tracking emerging high potential spaces ripe for preemptive positioning. Translate data into heat maps denoting target segments warranting strategic early moves in contrast with lagging legacy categories.

Assessing Contractual Impacts on Flexibility

Robust risk assessments weigh proposed terms against longer-term business flexibility since contractual constraints endure past initial deal lifecycles. Gauge limitations across critical facets like:

Intellectual Property: Overreaching rights assignments severely handicap technology innovation and product development capacities over multi-year horizons across entire market verticals.

Non-Compete Clauses: Agreements blocking other regional projects, adjacent segments, or public sector work may inflict major restrictions on growth well after contract expiration.

Data Rights: Broad claims governing access, usage rights, and exclusive controls over data generated when delivering solutions introduces future barriers on AI and analytics opportunities.

Flagging potentially damaging clauses early allows negotiation or decision trade-offs between revenue potential and strategic flexibility before signing binding agreements if unacceptable compromises emerge.

Model the Risk-Reward

Determining sound investments requires looking beyond immediate contract value by weighing multifaceted considerations around bid costs, delivery responsibilities, and expansion potential for judging long-range benefits justifying near-term expenditures.

Evaluating Bid Preparation Requirements

Securing RFP invitations hinges on conveying qualifications that meet established prequalification criteria related to past performance, financial stability, technical capabilities, quality certifications, security clearances and other gates screening for credible contenders with resources to fulfill stated needs.

If missing current credentials requires rapid capability advancement like new hires, facility investments or quick certifications, pursue only where sufficient win probability warrants expenditures based on contract value.

Bid preparation itself incurs additional costs around personnel hours across capture, proposal writing, subject matter reviews and leadership oversight. Further consider needs for external consulting support, market research purchases, printing, travel and other expenses tied directly to production.

Compare projected costs against the probability-adjusted contract value by multiplying the deal size by win odds percent. Set minimum thresholds where a 20% win likelihood on a $5M contract warrants no more than $1M in bid costs to ensure positive expected value.

Evaluating Post-Award Delivery Responsibilities

Beyond bid costs, successful awards incur contract delivery risks around fulfilling promised quality, timing, budgets, and contractual terms coupled with financial, technical and legal liabilities for non-compliance.

Gauge projected responsibilities across solution development, deployment, stabilization, transition and support activities requiring subject matter expertise, onsite facilities/equipment, and associated operating costs. Stress test against worst-case disruption scenarios.

Also project contract administration duties around invoicing, progress reporting, change orders and relationship management that consume management capacity over the delivery lifecycle.

Assessing Expansion Potential

An individual RFP may constitute just an initial foothold allowing much wider revenue potential from securing incumbent status for contract renewals, follow-on expansions and sole source work over 5-10 year time horizons. Assess possibilities around projected continuity needs spanning additional solutions, locations, portfolio integration and ongoing enhancements that require deep domain expertise.

This beachhead potential makes certain bids strategic springboards justifying heavier investments through long-term value well exceeding the initial scope. Carefully evaluate this stickiness power and determine where seed investments to anchor such ecosystems merit significant concessions or even loss leader positioning to win favors later.

Assessing Client Dynamics

Understanding RFP client complexity, familiarity through past engagements, and particular overseas nuances inform bid solutions targeting demonstrated pain points rather than misaligned offerings, set pragmatic expectations on internal consensus-building, anticipate offshore delivery intricacies, and gauge level of effort proportionate to contract value.

Profiling Decision-Making Complexity

Simple clients with concentrated authority require less upfront investment in consensus-building than multifaceted entities with dispersed influencers, convoluted procurement requiring alignment between distinct operating units, or situations complicated by separate funding sources, legacy tools stakeholders aim to safeguard, or specialized capability silos resistant to change.

Clarify the number of individual sign-offs needed across user groups, economic oversight committees, compliance supervisors, executive sponsors and other key players that builds realistic timelines. Also assess ease of navigating politics that could delay progress despite sponsor backing.

Past experiences deliver intuitions around navigating intricacies, or alternatively may reveal blindspots requiring third-party insights to decipher.

Factoring in Offshore Considerations

Overseas procurement layers on additional risk factors including unfavorable payment terms, currency complexities, import/export controls, cultural mismatches between client expectations and delivery region status quo, communications barriers that necessitate adaption like arranging local translators, client sensitivities requiring customized approaches, and steep learning curves grasping unique market norms without existing regional expertise.

Vetting prospective partner qualifications and track records serves imperative due diligence validating reputable standing, technical abilities, language proficiency, workplace culture affinity, communications infrastructure, necessary facilities and compliance rigor that inspires stakeholder trust in remote delivery models.

For example, a foreign outsourcer with sterling track record still necessitates revalidating their capability maturity that is aligned to local market standards rather than presuming seamless transferability to your market. Measure offshore risks against contract revenue potential and consider exceptions to global delivery models if requirements warrant it.

Carefully framing client dynamics, stakeholder complexity for securing internal consensus, likely procurement delays, need for regional partners, payment risks, location-specific change orders and other key considerations assists structuring terms and conditions commensurate with level of effort critical for overseas RFP success.

Assessing Organizational Readiness

Successfully delivering on RFP proposals requires having the right staffing, knowledge, and risk tolerance. Carefully judging current capabilities against demands in the bid is key to determining fit or identifying gaps needing investment.

Staffing and Resources

Compare existing team member skills and facilities against precise requirements in the bid across areas like:

- Staff credentials and specialized expertise

- Security clearance levels for sites

- Mandatory tools, software, equipment

Determine availability of personnel and budgets over needed time periods. Shortfalls may require new hires, contractors, rentals or purchases manageable within lead times. Develop plans addressing gaps upfront rather than assuming required resources.

Management Structure

Evaluate whether current executive focus allows sufficient leadership involvement given demands of the bid plus existing workloads. New opportunities may require assigning dedicated oversight like program managers or capture professionals to drive pursuit success.

Weigh taking on additional management hierarchy to support a new major contract against stretching resources too thin. Phase-in plans address interim gaps as organizations scale to support growth sustainably over time.

Requisite Experience

Gauge whether teams possess directly relevant past performance required or if knowledge gaps exist necessitating quick skill-building. Assess time and difficulty of acquiring technical certifications or soft skills like stakeholder management essential for quality delivery on compressed timelines.

Pursue only bids aligning with strategic roadmaps for capability advancement where timing buffers allow absorbing foreseeable learning curve delays without overwhelming staff.

Risk Assessments

Standard criteria weigh proposal complexity, payment terms favorability, team readiness and other risk factors against revenue potential and tolerance thresholds. Enforce formal approval gates before committing bids beyond acceptable risk levels.

Ongoing monitoring allows adjusting or ceasing efforts if indicators deteriorate. This governance ensures new contracts fitably align with organizational capacities as capabilities scale.

Chapter Five

Analyzing Your Competitors

C ompetitors rightly shield information that could undermine their
standing if revealed, making direct insights nearly impossible to obtain.
This requires competitive analysts to meticulously evaluate disparate indicators
and construct informed yet imperfect understandings of opponents' capabilities, limitations, and likely approaches.

Piecemealing together a mosaic of assessments from scattered publicly available
clues is preferable to bidding without any perspective on the field. Minor visibility, even if incomplete, allows more strategic counterpositioning than complete
blindness.

A variety of sources provide pieces of the competitive puzzle. Thorough examination of annual reports, industry presentations, and other public disclosures
can expose subtle changes to rivals' priorities, finances, or marketed solutions
that signal positional adaptations. Conversations with former employees, common partners, or industry contacts may provide unverified but suggestive intelligence on emerging internal dynamics or project ambitions.

Analyzing historical patterns in how competitors reacted to parallel situations
offers probabilistic projections of coming moves. For example, regularly de-

fending flagship products aggressively indicates fierce resistance could greet new complementary offerings. Weak past responses to niche threats hints at vulnerable flanks attracting more extensive feature matching this cycle.

Of course, no single input provides an entirely conclusive or comprehensive profile. But systematically gathering and cross-referencing indicators across multiple sources allows crafting working hypotheses of relative strengths, strategic foci, cultural tendencies, and go-to-playbooks.

Structured analytical processes then quantitatively estimate win likelihoods against reconstructed competitive landscapes. Metrics like capability alignments, relationship synergies, market momentum, and resource efficiency factor into calculated probabilities of securing new prospects.

Proportioning development investments to plausibility assessments optimizes returns given risk. Conservative or heavyweight commitments suit longshot or favored bids respectively. Ongoing intel assimilation refines perspectives, triggering adjustments that maximize value realization over portfolio results.

Though founded on inference rather than direct visibility, an evidence-based competitive framework better allocates efforts than reactive scrambling. It strengthens strategic positioning through proactive rather than passive competition. Competitive intelligence fills crucial blindspots that hinder effectiveness, yielding substantial advantages through prudent strategy.

The Challenges of Direct Competitor Intelligence

Ideally, comprehensive real-time insight into rival pricing formulas, positional vulnerabilities, resourcing constraints, technology roadmaps, and win-loss motivations would optimize counterproposals. However, competitors purposefully restrict access to such vital details to trusted insiders only on a need-to-know basis.

Directly inserting oneself into a competitor's decision-making inner workings presents clear practical and ethical challenges that are difficult to overcome. While espionage-like scenarios depicted in entertainment can seem thrilling, they rarely unfold in the real business world. Even if such sensitive materials were somehow accessed, the information would quickly become outdated as strategies shift to address constantly evolving market conditions.

Furthermore, data taken out of context and without expert analysis risks spreading misperceptions more than useful insights. A more constructive approach acknowledges information asymmetries while leveraging publicly available clues and inferences to understand the landscape well enough to compete effectively. The strategic considerations around competitive intelligence gathering warrant a balanced, ethical perspective focused on proactive strategies rather than reactionary tactics.

Alternative Competitor Intelligence Gathering

Gathering intelligence about competitors indirectly can provide useful insights when direct observation is limited:

Public Disclosures: Securities filings, corporate reports, press releases – especially shifted messaging – suggest responses to financial results and strategic reprioritizations.

Industry Connections: Conversations with common supply chain partners, former employees, trade journal friends potentially reveal insider rumors (if not definitive actions).

Past Behavior Patterns: Historical responses to parallel competitive situations indicate behavioral tendencies projected as probable future moves.

No single source provides a full picture. But identifying aligned signals across multiple incomplete sources allows building sufficient perspective to guide effective responses.

It's also important to distinguish between intentional misdirections meant to distract and actual meaningful hints about intentions. Not all indicators reliably reflect a competitor's true positioning or planned moves. Careful analysis separates strategic feints from real reveals behind competitors' actions.

Key Insights For Bid Decisions

While exhaustive competitor dossiers prove implausible, focused intelligence gathering priorities will inform critical considerations:

Count of Credible Rivals: How many competitors boast technical capabilities actually meeting requirements? Financially stable to deliver without risk? Familiar relationships with the buyer? Filtering for quality narrows the field to genuine threats.

Historical Win Rates: Which shortlisted contenders consistently win similar contracts? Dark horse bidders sometimes surprise but informed probabilities predict usual suspects. Track records estimate relative formidability.

Economic Motivations: Who urgently needs this revenue? Incumbents losing accounts aggressively rebid to replace losses. Cash strapped players cut margins bidding for lifelines. Assess bidder hunger. Desperation signals generosity.

While other factors matter, even crude directional signals on these above considerations can assist in forecasting competitor moves.

Bid Investments Aligned to Favorability

Limited visibility into competitors unavoidably injects uncertainty into perfectly predicting competitor actions. However, insight enables probabilistic models gauging situational favorability to determine proportional bid investments.

If the competitive field appears fairly level among suitable bidders, estimate the chance of winning as roughly equal to the number of bidders. When the likelihood of success is low, keep costs below expected returns. If relationships or strengths indicate significant advantages versus clearly weaker opponents, increase development spending up to analyzed maximum values.

While the fog of war always obscures battlefields, thoughtful competitive intelligence peering into the mist provides sufficient visibility to inform wise commitments aligned to favorable conditions for victory.

Chapter Six

Analyzing the RFP Documents

When preparing a bid for a contract, it is important to carefully review all the documents provided by the client. These documents contain valuable details to help you understand what is required.

The client will give bidders a tender package with the necessary bidding materials. This package may have a name like Request for Proposal, Invitation to Tender, or Project Brief. It will provide information about the work being requested as well as instructions for submitting your bid.

Pay close attention to any Instructions to Tenderers. Here the client lays out important rules about how your bid needs to be formatted and what to include. Failing to follow these instructions exactly could hurt your chances of winning. You may also receive guidance notes from the client. These explain their process and preferences in plain language. Make sure to address all topics they request and in the way they specify. The guidance notes also share how bids will be evaluated.

Be thorough - read all materials multiple times. Refer back to the tender package as you develop your bid to ensure compliance. Check for any extra documents attached that offer useful context about strategies, policies or technical details.

While the client provides this information for your use, verify important facts independently if possible. Clients may note tender materials are intended to help but bidders must do their own research.

Taking the time to fully understand client requirements up front through the tender documents is key to crafting a competitive, compliant proposal and avoiding disqualification down the road. Let the package be your guide throughout the bidding process.

Bid Submission Requirements

One of the most important aspects of responding to a tender is ensuring your bid complies with all of the client's submission instructions. Failure to adhere to the specified requirements could result in disqualification from the bidding process. Therefore, it is imperative that bidders thoroughly review this section of the tender documentation.

Content Format

The submission criteria will provide guidance on structuring the content and format of the bid document itself. This may include stipulations around page limits, font sizes, sections to be included, and more. Organizing the proposal according to the prescribed structure is crucial, as deviation could cause the bid to be rejected outright. Tender documents will also specify whether bids must be submitted electronically or in hard copy, as well as the number of required copies.

Packaging and Labeling

Equally important are the packaging and labeling expectations. The tender will detail how bids should be packaged for delivery and identify marks or labels that must be affixed. This could include instructions to submit proposals in sealed envelopes or boxes marked with identifying information like the tender number or bidder's name. Meeting bagging and tagging specifications demonstrates attention to detail.

Delivery Method

Directions must also be followed for actually delivering bids to the client by the specified date and time. Common requirements include hand delivery versus postal service, cut-off thresholds for late bids, and confirmation protocols. Bidders should confirm arrangements like delivery addresses, instructions for special handling, and requirements for receipts or notifications. Showing up past deadlines or with incomplete documentation can scupper an otherwise qualified proposal.

Supporting Documents

Supporting documentation including forms, templates, budgets and declarations should likewise match any formats provided by the client. Signing and returning requested agreements upfront signals willingness to be bound should the bid win. Pricing and commercial submissions especially rely on grids and cost models that necessitate precise population. Failure to use prescribed mechanisms can undermine the evaluation process.

While response content forms the crux of bids, disregarding framework factors renders all efforts moot. Careful compliance with the discrete yet pivotal submission criteria outlined helps ensure bids actually get reviewed on their merits instead of dismissed due to technicalities. Following tender instructions to the letter ultimately better positions proposals going into evaluation.

Understanding the Client

To craft an effective proposal, it is important for bidders to first comprehend who the client is as an organization. A thorough review of background details provided in the tender documents helps illuminate the client's structure and operations.

Key information to gather includes the client's origins, size, and operational dimensions. Notes should be made of any partnerships, boards, committees, or other entities also involved. Identification of specific departments or divisions engaging in the procurement process provides context.

Equally vital is discerning who the ultimate decision makers will be. Titles, roles, and names of individuals managing or influencing the evaluation and selection should be recorded. Understanding these stakeholders' positions within the client organization assists in properly aligning and emphasizing the proposal.

Contact details listed can form the basis for follow up inquiries to gain further insights. While clients aim to provide a transparent overview, additional clarity benefits both parties. Comprehension of internal politics and different perspectives held lay the foundation for establishing rapport with assessors.

Determining Objectives

Clearly defined objectives and intended outcomes represent the core purpose behind any tender. Bidders must ascertain the client's goals to develop solutions correctly addressing needs.

Thorough review checks for consistent, credible high-level statements of what the client hopes to accomplish. Bid responses then directly link delivered capabilities and benefits to furthering the expressed objectives.

Inconsistencies across documentation warrant scrutiny, as mixed objectives risk solutions pleasing some needs but not others. Any apparent lack of grasp regarding envisioned outcomes by the client also bears examination. Consultation may help refine objectives for mutual understanding.

Expanding Comprehension

When objectives remain unclear, external research expands the picture. Investigating the client's website and annual reports provides strategic context.

Discussing the opportunity with existing vendors, partners or client contacts offers new angles.

Indirect questioning during site tours or demonstrations tests objectives without direct queries. Probing understandably centers discussion to deduce the functional requirements driving procurement.

No assumption replaces direct contact however. Respectfully inquiring through Client Relationship Managers presents opportunities introducing specialized domain knowledge and insights aligning exactly to priorities.

Supplemental research and diplomatic engagement optimize response fit without appearing distrustful of supplied materials. Outreach deepens relationships and comprehension crucial for accurate targeting of solutions proposed.

Thorough review coupled with respectful inquiries ensures bids accurately reflect a client's true needs, structure and decision-making dynamics. Background evaluations and Objective validations form the basis for strategic positioning catered to each client's unique requirements and procurement journey.

Evaluating Technical Requirements

Thoroughly examining the scope of services forms a basis for determining commitment levels. Bidders assess whether specifications clearly define deliverables in a way simplifying translation into action plans and resourcing needs.

It's important to understand all the work that needs to be done. The client needs to clearly explain what is required, and this is usually found in the tender documents. If any parts are unclear or vague, ask questions. This prevents problems later on. Make notes about things that will take a lot of time and effort versus routine tasks. Pay attention to minor details too - they may reveal the true priorities.

Check that nothing important was left out accidentally. The client should directly say what is excluded to avoid assumptions. Clear up any gray areas about responsibilities to avoid arguments later.

Figure out which tasks are simple and which need special skills or experience. More complex parts may need experts or extra time to complete the work. Simpler work can be assigned to other staff.

It's helpful to break down the entire project into smaller pieces. This helps estimate how long each part will take and the resources required. For example, some sections may only take a few days while others require weeks of effort. Understanding the project in this level of detail is important from the beginning. Asking questions upfront prevents surprises later. Taking thorough notes on the scope of work allows for accurate planning and preparation of the proposal.

This better positions bids to meet all client needs.

Division of Responsibilities

It's important to understand who will do what if more than one company is involved. When a few companies work together, the client needs to be clear about each one's job.

If responsibilities are not sorted out early on, things could get mixed up or people may blame each other later. Gaps where no one takes charge of certain tasks could cause quality issues and delays, forcing the client to step in.

Upfront documents should separate the hand-offs clearly between companies. This formalizes expectations and helps with cooperation between groups working together.

External Influences

Regulations, laws and standard industry practices affect how work can be performed. Learning the rules prevents offering solutions that don't comply.

Constraints like budgets and timelines from outside the project also impact what can realistically be promised. Understanding influences ahead of time enables adjusting plans as outside conditions change over long projects.

Methodology Requirements

Guidance on processes, whether standard or customized, aids tailoring the approach. Using preferred methods makes the transition smoother.

Limits on options need identification of acceptable workarounds that still meet requirements. Distinguishing requirements from suggestions avoids non-approved solutions, like when alternatives better meet needs.

Fully grasping responsibilities, rules and methods upfront aids determining needs and creative solutions aligned with the true scope of work. Asking questions early on leads to stronger proposals.

Information Requirements

One of the most important parts of proposal preparation is ensuring all submission requirements are carefully addressed. Bidders must closely follow any formats, templates or categorization schema provided by the client. Standardization streamlines comparison between bids and demonstrates a contractor's ability to adhere to stipulated documentation protocols. Deviating from the established structure risks proposals receiving penalties or outright rejection during evaluation.

In addition to structural elements, clients will specifically request certain details, content or supporting documents be included. Proposal responses must supply fully fleshed out answers to all required sections like technical designs, project plans, timelines or staffing levels and qualifications to satisfy assessors. Any omissions leave evaluators lacking information necessary for fair consideration against competitors. Bid submissions should address each information point raised to avoid disqualification on technicalities.

Directives related to volume or length of content must likewise be strictly honored. Indicated page limits guard against excessively wordy or expansive responses, maintaining focus on succinctly hitting high priority highlights. Respecting quantity constraints also exhibits respect for busy reviewers' time. If page allotments feel too narrow, early inquiry for reasonable extension avoids hasty culling or abbreviation jeopardizing quality.

Some solicitation packages even provide sample or template documents to populate. Precisely entering financial calculations, resource allocations or solution blueprints into supplied worksheets streamlines assessors' digesting commercial and functional fitness. Additional branding or contextual data may complement mandated information through executive summaries, value propositions and selection rationales promoting competitive differentiators.

Outside supplemental materials substantiate claims. Referencing third party industry awards, client testimonials or case studiesbolsters credibility on capabilities and track record. Organizing supporting files compliantly mirrors established submission instructions. Inquiries clarify any ambiguous requirements before proposals are finalized, avoiding unpleasant surprises from incomplete responses displeasing clients.

Overall, while content forms the core function of bids, overlooking framework factors surrounding presentation renders efforts potentially futile. Suppliers displaying diligent adherence to information needs through coherent, meticulously-assembled proposals demonstrate reliability and attention to detail prized by customers. Compliance better positions contractors as serious partners worthy of serious consideration for contract awards.

Priorities and Competitiveness

Gaining insight into the client's true intentions helps craft optimally targeted responses. Bidders should discern emphasized and overlooked matters beyond surface-level documentation. Questions beyond evident pain points uncover needs demanding resolution.

Assessing Strengths and Weaknesses

It's important to look at your own strengths and weaknesses before submitting your proposal. Think about what you're good at and what areas could be better.

Your proposal should focus on the strengths that match up best with what the client seems to want most, based on what you've learned from the tender documents. Play up your advantages that relate directly to their priorities. Also consider any weak points and how to improve them. Look for ways to minimize or make up for weaknesses that could hurt your chances of winning. Come up with strategies in your bid to address weaknesses.

Identifying both strengths and areas for progress within your own submission helps you showcase what's most relevant for the client. It also shows you understand your own abilities and are actively working to provide the best possible solution. Evaluating different parts of your bid allows you to target it directly to the client's needs and priorities.

Authenticating Priorities

To understand the client's true priorities, look at what areas get more attention and discussion versus brief mentions.

Things covered in more depth and detail are probably real focuses, not just minor points. On the other hand, overlooked topics likely don't matter as much even if not mentioned much.

Pay attention to whether important-sounding things are just listed or whether there are real questions and inquiries showing interest. The level of interest compared to things briefly covered or skipped can reveal what really needs to be addressed.

You need to validate what you think the priorities are based on depth of coverage versus shallow mentions. This helps point your solution in the right direction to meet what matters most to the client instead of lesser concerns. Properly identifying the genuine priorities directs how to shape your proposal.

Pitching Differentiation

Once you figure out the top priorities, focus your proposal on clearly meeting those needs. Showcase how your strengths match up perfectly to address the most important areas.

Highlight past successes that far surpass what the client expects to get from proposals. This sets you apart from other bidders.

Emphasize your advantages that are centered on the top priorities. Also address any weaknesses by explaining your solutions.

Positioning your bid this way, with emphasis on the priorities, maximizes how persuasive it will be. Highlighting exceptional performance in the most important subjects gives you an edge over competing bids. Proving you truly meet the client's sincere driving forces strengthens your bid's appeal.

Required Qualifications

Thorough examination of preferred qualifications gives insight into criteria bids will be assessed against. Tender documentation outlines technical skills, sector knowledge, and contextual experience valued by the client. Make sure to note explicitly stated requirements as well as desirable traits that may offer competitive advantage. Supplementary research on industry trends and client organization norms provides additional perspective.

Project Team Composition

It's important to understand what type and how many people the client needs for the project team. The bid should specify positions, roles, and experience levels required.

The number of people gives you an idea of the scale of work involved. Designated roles help with assigning the right resources to each job. You may also need to work together with client staff or partner with other companies. Getting clear on joint work arrangements is key as it impacts how people interact.

Thinking about the team makeup early allowsaligning your available people to fulfill expected roles. Advance planning helpsensure your proposed team fitswhat's requested and streamlinesthe approval process. Properly addressing project team compositionshows you comprehend resource needsto complete the work successfully.

Addressing Logistical Requirements

It's important to consider any logistical requirements to do the job, like offices, equipment, vehicles and location of work. These logistics are important for fulfilling what's required.

Pay attention to what resources like facilities and tools the client specifies. Make sure you can provide or easily get access to the mandated items. There may also be side effects to think about, such as organizing transportation or relying on other companies. These dependencies are worth considering for feasibility.

Visiting sites in person, if practical, helps gain real understanding of logistical factors. First-hand looks at premises provide useful context behind requirements such as space, accessibility, or security among others.

Examining logistical demands and provisions thoroughly demonstrates understanding all that's required practically to complete the work successfully on the ground.

Mitigation Strategies

Mandatory requirements set the minimum level of requirements that you need to meet, but some minor weaknesses can still be solved. It's better to identify these and propose remedies than risk automatic rejection.

Have backup plans ready to show how you'll handle possible shortfalls or contingencies that arise. Arguments for similar or extra steps can still meet the intent, even if not exact matches.

Showing you understand risks and are ready to tackle issues proactively strengthens your bid over being dismissed on small technicalities. Comprehensively mitigating potential problems boosts your chances versus exclusion for trivial reasons. Addressing areas that may fall slightly short demonstrates initiative instead of assuming problems can't be fixed. Equivalent solutions or supplemental actions back up your ability to adequately fulfill what's required.

Proposal Validation

Weigh your skills and proposal against the client's must-haves. Spot any gaps that could cause issues if not resolved.

Variances don't mean you're out, but do require solutions to reassure ability. Differences also open chances to add more value. Refine details like resources, work scope, or cost savings to demonstrate your commitment to needs. Getting client input helps really learn the important factors.

Thorough validation strengthens proposals as fully meeting job requirements. Showing gaps get fixed exhibits proactivity, while validation seals compliance to criteria. Satisfying predetermined standards makes you eligible for favorable review.

Careful examination informs customizing bids as qualified for the work. Addressing issues and verifying all is covered sets quality proposals for best chance at winning.

Subcontracting

Check if the client allows parts of the work to be done by other companies you hire (called subcontractors). Follow any rules about how much can be given to subcontractors versus doing it yourself.

Some clients limit how much of the total project can be assigned to subcontractors, so make sure your proposal is within those bounds. You may need approval for certain types of work to be done by others. The tender documents should say if you need to directly provide information about subcontractors you plan to use. This helps the client assess the capabilities of all companies involved in completing the project.

Be ready to disclose details such as the names of subcontractors, their experience level, and the specific parts of the work they will handle if required. Provide this subcontractor information upfront with your initial bid.

Ensure any subcontractors you list are willing and able to do the work at the price quoted as you'll be responsible for their performance, so carefully selecting qualified help is important.

Using subcontractors lets you supplement your capabilities. But you still need to manage the project yourself and take full responsibility for quality. Make certain to thoroughly screen subcontractors and clearly define each party's responsibilities in any contracts.

Methodology

Take note of any specific procedures or methods specified by the client as mandatory to follow. Pay close attention to any standards, workflows, or policies described that must be adhered to in your proposal.

Carefully record these required procedures, as following the client's stipulated methodology is essential. Deviating from their stated expectations risks non-compliance and rejection of your bid.

Allowable Variations

Find out if the client will consider alternative approaches to their prescribed methodology. Many still require a conforming solution to be proposed first before variants may augment the core approach.

If variations could strengthen your bid, identify exactly what flexibility is permitted. Note any qualifications stated around modified methods - some room for variants doesn't mean a completely different solution will satisfy the client.

Ask for clarification of conditions under which the client finds customized approaches acceptable. Additional approval may be needed to use variations from written procedures. Establishing allowable flexibility avoids non-conforming strategy selection.

Tailoring the Solution

With regulatory allowances understood, examine how best to structure your methodology to address the project. A four-step process ensures alignment:

1. Propose the requested core approach in full, demonstrating capability and intent to satisfy as priority.

2. Identify proposed variants to standardized workflows, providing solid rationale linking customizations to increased value.

3. Qualify all tailored aspects as meeting stated conditions for approved flexibility from specifications.

4. Highlight advantages of variants while still honoring mandated procedural requirements and preferences expressed.

Confirming Methodology Fit

Validating solution fit establishes prospective viability. Compare full methodology against tender criteria, uncovering potential gaps needing remedy. Discrepancies risk dismissal, necessitating resolution strategies like:

- Equivalent alternatives meeting intended outcomes if not exact steps

- Supplemental procedures bridging variances

- Refined scoping to alleviate nonconforming aspects

Addressing variances exhibits commitment to compliance while variants showcase value-added innovation. Client check-ins facilitate continuing education on fit and optimization of proprietary methodology design. Comprehensive validation achieves fully qualified solution proposals.

Proposed methodologies are most compelling adhering to core needs while customized elements add distinguishable value, all through meticulous confirmation of fitness for client and project requirements.

Risk Management

It's important to address how you'll deal with risks and uncertainties that could affect the project. Take note of any risk management processes, actions, or tools the client expects to see in your proposal.

Common requirements involve creating a risk register or risk matrix to log possible dangers. This demonstrates understanding of risks rather than ignoring hazards. Carefully follow template formats if the client supplies sample registers. The register should record risk identification, analysis and response planning. Estimate likelihood and impact of each risk occurring with mitigation applied. Assign ownership of monitored risks to responsible parties.

Determine probabilities and consequences numerically or descriptively. Rate risks green, yellow or red based on criteria to focus priorities. Develop contingency plans per risk level with prevention and recovery strategies.

Specify risk sharing arrangements clearly. Note which risks your company takes responsibility for resolving versus shared risks both parties must manage cooperatively. Outline financial responsibilities for each risk category too. Validate comprehensiveness of your risk approach. Include all potential hazards implied or directly mentioned as concerns. Subject matter experts provide additional insight on industry or project-specific uncertainties. Review risk planning thoroughly.

Addressing uncertainties proactively reassures ability to handle unexpected issues. Following client expectations demonstrates understanding of importance in carefully risk assessment and mitigation throughout the project lifecycle.

Project Schedule

Study the scope of work - everything that needs to be done on the project as described in the RFP. Figure out if the schedule allows enough total time to realistically accomplish all the tasks involved. Some things to consider are how complex each task is and how long each one might take your team. Make sure you have factored in adequate time for any testing, reviews, revisions or approval processes required by the client.

The client's schedule might not account for the time it takes them to review deliverables from your team and provide feedback. Projects often need adjustments along the way. So consider adding more time buffers to the schedule to allow for this back and forth with the client. If the schedule seems too tight after reviewing the scope thoroughly, your team risks rushing work or missing deadlines.

When drafting your proposal response, you can note if you have any concerns about the timeframe. Estimate your own schedule based on the scope and your experience. Adjusting expectations upfront helps set realistic goals and prevents potential problems later in project execution.

Comparing Timelines to Work Outputs

Match up the timeline with the actual work that needs to be completed. This means comparing the deliverables or outputs required against how much time is allotted for each stage of the project.

Carefully examine what exactly needs to be produced by the schedule's milestone dates. Make sure the timing allows your team to reasonably finish each deliverable. Watch out for mismatches, like a deliverable that seems too complex being due too soon.

Some key things to look at are how frequent deliverables are expected and how much work each one represents. Be sure the schedule realistically accommodates the content, testing, approval time etc needed for the pieces of work.

If you notice certain deliverables may be difficult to finish on time, take note of these potential risks. Discuss your concerns with the client, explaining why the timing seems unrealistic for those specific tasks. You may need to adjust either the expected content or the completion dates to make the plan actually feasible.

By thoroughly lining up deliverables and deadlines, you can confidently assess if the overall pace is achievable. Bring any mismatches to the client's attention early on so the schedule can be made reasonable if changes are needed. This helps set the project timeline for effective planning and avoids issues down the road.

Progress Reporting Requirements

Also note any obligations for regular progress updates to the client as these will factor into the manpower and skill requirements. Frequent check-ins add to the work needed, so consider this when planning resources.

Identify reporting formats, how often updates are expected, and what must be included. Common examples are written status reports, demonstration meetings, or feedback forms. Make sure your team has the ability and available bandwidth for these check-ins.

Determine if in-person meetings or calls are mandatory at certain milestones. Reserve the appropriate time for prepping, attending and recapping meetings on your project calendar. Verify you have staff with communication skills fit for client discussions.

Also note that changes impacting schedules must be agreed upon with the client. Make it clear from the outset that shifting deadlines requires their approval. This sets realistic expectations that timelines may require adjustment as the project evolves.

When finalizing your proposed schedule, aim for balance between feasibility on your end and addressing the client's needs. Run the schedule by the client for validation before signing on. Direct communication at this stage optimizes understanding between parties.

Project Budget

Consider whether the budget fits the work that needs to be done. Take a close look at the scope of the project and carefully estimate what it will realistically cost your company to complete all the tasks and deliverables.

Evaluate factors like the staffing levels required, estimated hours for each role, any travel or materials expected, and additional costs for unforeseen work. Compare your estimated budget to the amount provided in the client's proposal documents.

If there appears to be a mismatch, with the client's budget coming in too low, take note of this potential issue. Thoroughly assessing the budget implications early prevents problems later.

Bring any budget concerns directly to the client before submitting your estimate. Explain why the money allotted may not cover your projected costs to do the job well. This opens a discussion for adjusting either the budget amount or reducing the project scope as needed.

Adopting an upfront, collaborative approach ensures all parties have feasible expectations. With clear communication, acceptable solutions can be found before moving forward to the estimating process. Avoiding low budgets protects both your company and the client from unrealistic timelines or missed quality standards down the road.

Breaking Down Costs Over Time

When estimating costs for a project, it helps to break down projected expenses over the different stages of the schedule.

Take the total estimated budget you calculated and spread it across the timeline segments used in the project plan. Match costs to the phases where work will occur and deliverables are due. This provides a view of how the budgeted money will be spent steadily throughout the project. For example, you may have higher expenses in the beginning design phase compared to later development stages.

Presenting cost projections broken out by the schedule's intervals demonstrates a thorough spending plan to the client. It allows them to see how funds will be applied at each milestone. If segments of the timeline need adjustment after reviewing your cost breakdown, that can be addressed up front. Breaking out expenses brings any mismatches between budget allocation and work phases to light early.

Distributing estimated spending routinely across the schedule supports realistic financial planning. It ensures the client understands when fees will be incurred. Any concerns over fit between cash flow and work flow can then be discussed proactively with the client.

Formulating Your Cost Estimate

Tally expected direct costs such as materials, the hours each team member will work at their hourly rate, any equipment rental fees, and payments to outside contractors or vendors.

Additionally, factor in overhead costs such as office space, utilities, and support staff time not directly billable to the project. Also account for your desired profit margin. Be sure to present these figures in an organized format that is clear and easy for the client to understand. While comprehensive, keep the estimate concise.

Most importantly, show that your proposed work can be completed at or under the budget amount provided. Demonstrate efficiency by submitting a cost-effective estimate that delivers full value for the client's investment.

Validate your estimate falls within budgetary constraints before submission. Striving for maximum work output relative to funds allotted strengthens your proposal's competitiveness. Taking the time to articulate all projected fees in a transparent, accessible estimate builds confidence that the project budget will be well-managed from start to finish.

Verify Estimate is Feasible

Double check that your projected pricing accurately accounts for all labor, materials, overhead costs and other expenses required to fulfill the entire project scope.

Confirm that your team can realistically accomplish all deliverables at the total estimated budget level while maintaining a reasonable profit margin. Make any necessary adjustments to your costing model and reevaluate the estimates.

Take time to ensure your proposed pricing aligns logically with both the client's stated budget and the planned project timeline. Careful evaluation is needed to optimize viability.

Estimates seen as unrealistic may discourage consideration, so correlation amongst costs, budgets and schedules should be clearly justified. Adopting a meticulous assessment approach demonstrates your commitment to afford-ability and feasibility. Only proposed estimates that are thoroughly verified can confidently be presented as financially sustainable for your business to take on the work.

Selection Process and Contract Evaluation

When bidding for a contract, it is critical to understand what factors the client prioritizes in selecting a vendor, and the decision criteria weighting. This pro-vides key insight into aligning your proposal for the best chance of winning.

Specifically, note the relative importance placed on qualitative factors assessing the merit of your technical solution versus quantitative price points in the scoring methodology.

Qualitative criteria typically examine strengths matching client needs like rel-evant past performance and subject matter expertise. Assessments delve into capability depth across solution domains directly pertinent to fulfilling their unique requirements.

In contrast, quantitative scoring weighs pricing factors like the overall bid bud-get, rate cards mapping hourly fees for defined roles, and total cost projections based on scoping key delivery milestones. These estimate expected expenditures investing in your solution.

Ideally, request clarity around rating scales, minimum thresholds, and deci-sion committee structures governing evaluations if public methodologies lack transparency. Probing the underlying selection values drives requirements pri-oritization when tailoring differentiated proposals for maximum impact given decision maker hot buttons and conceptions of value beyond pure bottom line costs.

Carefully studying solicitation evaluation frameworks spotlights where to concentrate proposal development efforts between demonstrating technical sophistication in line with needs or structuring financially attractive packages prioritized as decisive in final selections.

Valued Evaluation Elements

Carefully study RFP scoring methodologies to identify specific capability elements and attributes defined as highly valuable by the client. Emphasizing proposal responses directly targeting these priority aspects boosts competitiveness.

For example, an RFP may weight customized innovations tailored to their unique use cases over generic blanket solutions. In this case, strongly showcase specialized offerings purpose-built around their niche needs rather than stretching standardized products misaligned with scenarios.

Likewise, the methodology may favor flexible delivery models easily adapted to future growth or emerging requirements through transparent change processes versus rigid implementation plans resistant to modifications. Accordingly, detail change control mechanisms, showcase past agility scaling solutions upwards, and promise accommodating models.

If environmental sustainability tops selection criteria, thoroughly document related practices in areas like materials sourcing, carbon footprints tracking, electronic waste recycling policies and responsible water use. Prominently feature achievements in Corporate Social Responsibility reports.

Carefully aligning proposal elements against explicitly defined evaluation priorities signals close listening to customer needs. Flagging desired hallmarks displayed prominently indicates readiness fulfilling expectations around capabilities deemed critically differentiating value. This direct match gains advantage over generic, one-size-fits-none proposals miscalibrating weighted decision factors.

Thoughtfully personalized responses resonating with reviewers through tailored understanding of needs counters impersonal commodity-like bids appearing transactional rather than consultative.

Partnership Factors

Certain contracts center on extensive collaboration between vendor and client organizations. Carefully assess if the RFP methodology weighs team integration enablers as critical evaluation factors for these joint efforts.

Specifically, note any emphasis placed on demonstrated partnership capabilities regarding team cohesion cultivated through trust-building, clear communication norms, tightly-coordinated workflows, transparent progress tracking and unified culture.

The solicitation may favor proposals prominently featuring elements like:

- Governance structures with integrated planning committees allowing collaborative guidance on requirements, schedules and issue resolution

- Liaison roles directly bridging teams via agreed information flows, quick feedback loops and relationship management prioritization

- Digital tools, platforms and portals enabling transparent project visibility continuously across parties through centralized access to plans, dashboards, documents and generative discussions

- CodifiedFlexible partnership principles focused on openness, patience and good faith problem-solving

Readiness showcasing interoperability with existing systems, noted experience smoothly integrating while protecting current investments, and cultural affinities easing connections similarly demonstrate credible collaboration postures.

Heightened sensitivity aligning solutions, language and positioned team attributes to explicitly encouraged selection criteria builds affinity with client priorities seeking partners matching desired cooperative profiles critical for mutual success pursuing ambitious shared goals.

Examining Contract Terms

Carefully reviewing full contract drafts as early as possible familiarizes teams with proposed terms well before signing. This proactive alignment identifies deviations from norms that warrant evaluation.

Specifically note provisions diverging from standard industry agreements in your region across areas like payment procedures, liability clauses, intellectual property controls or requirements ownership. Mark unfamiliar terms lacking contextual precedents for probing. Likewise flag clauses introducing potential delivery risks beyond current capabilities or capacities without modifications, such as:

- Overly narrow deadlines unable to accommodate unforeseen delays

- Burdensome SLAs severely penalizing minor defects

- Restrictive staffing prerequisites limiting flexibility

- Onerous security prerequisites increasing overheads

- Excessive liability levels jeopardizing operations

Schedule formal reviews to address questions, clarify uncertainties, negotiate adjustments or secure approvals for any problematic provisions surfaced. Proactively resolving contract concerns prevents downstream disputes from unclear expectations or surprise obligations agreed hastily without properly gauging organizational fit.

Standard Contract Review

Even when contracts largely reflect typical terms and conditions, diligently validate full comprehension of proposed commitments prior to finalization to enable educated decisions protecting interests. Specifically, note details around common boilerplate provisions with substantial operational or financial implications like:

Payment Timelines: Invoice schedules, retention amounts withheld pending milestones, and exact due dates. Late payments hamper cash flows.

Insurance/Indemnity: Required liability coverage types and levels carrying premium expenses. Indemnification obligations introduce unforeseen costs from legal claims.

Termination Clauses: Non-performance criteria triggering dissolution allowing unpaid cancelation despite sunk efforts.

IP Ownership: Provisions governing intellectual property and proprietary elements developed during projects, restricting future licensing opportunities.

Warranties: Post-delivery defect correction requirements mandating free maintenance or replacement components over set periods.

While reviewing formal contracts seems routine, assumptions risk overlooking material issues. Checklists prevent oversights Flag unfamiliar provisions. Verify interpretations of standards with advisors to determine acceptable exposure given historical norms.

Confirming exact implications avoids blind spots. Pausing paperwork to ensure diligent mutual understanding on complex legal terminology prevents downstream disputes from mismatches between expectations and obligations.

Variance Consideration

When RFP contracts contain non-standard terms deviating from industry norms, closely evaluate the feasibility and impact of complying with these unique stipulations prior to finalization.

First, gauge the ability to operationally meet atypical performance requirements considering current capacities across resources, capabilities, and risk tolerances. Quantify any necessary investment tradeoffs to fulfill special conditions at acceptable quality levels. For example, requirements for onshore staffing mandates hiring otherwise offshored roles locally at higher costs. Exceptionally narrow delivery timelines necessitate expensive surge staffing unable to be sustained long-term. Hyper-stringent Service Level Agreemtents (SLAs) multiply project management overhead.

Next, financially model the exact margin and cash flow consequences imposed by unusual demands in areas like more frequent payment milestones, retention held longer, expanded liability guarantees, or additional reporting needs. Estimate impacts on financial planning.

Finally, escalate concerns around any problematic provisions misaligned with organizational realities for further dialogue given unviable conditions or disproportionate constraints. Explore adjustments or alternative solutions suitably addressing core interests without overextending capabilities.

Open and honest negotiations aim to find common ground between the initial contract offer and what we feel able to agree to. Seeking fair compromises demonstrates goodwill and a desire for a long-term partnership, rather than just a one-time transaction. The goal is to reach mutual understanding on terms that meet the reasonable needs of both parties.

Contract Agreement

Directly acknowledge and confirm all non-standard or otherwise concerning contract elements surfaced during RFP reviews within written bids to signal diligent scrutinization and invite prospective negotiations.

Specifically call out unusual provisions related to payment protocols, expansive liability clauses, restrictive staffing mandates, onerous security prerequisites or extensive maintenance obligations that exceed norms. Referencing issues early directly in proposals opens doors resolving complications proactively rather than encountering unworkable terms post-award after investments make walking away painful despite untenable conditions.

Surface-level confirmation statements demonstrate review without appearing confrontational. For example, gently flag extended liability provisions requesting future discussion given material deviation from customary levels manageable within typical operating models. This prompts amenable dialogue.

Proposing teams still emphasize satisfying defined RFP evaluation factors above debating legal minutiae. Competitive responses directly address scoped requirements through persuasive value propositions aligned with core selection criteria weighted towards technical solutions, demonstrated competencies, client fit and cultural affinities that compel award on merits.

However, briefly acknowledging contract elements warranting attention signals awareness defending partner interests parallel to touting qualifications. This balanced posture blends competitive positioning with principles assessing workability. RFP winners convince reviewers of organizational excellence while stewarding relationships evidenced by proactive contract considerations seeking mutual benefit. Cross-validating compliance and concern forestalls downstream disputes from today's unknown unknowns while still effectively showcasing partner potential.

Chapter Seven

Developing a Winning RFP Response

C lients overwhelmingly prefer RFP responses that directly address requirements with clear, succinct messaging rather than excessive documentation. More pages do not equate to a superior proposal. Excess length risks
clouding persuasive value propositions diluted across tangents diverting from
core strengths matching prioritized needs.

Many RFPs mandate strict page limits and content guidelines forcing concise
positioning. Rigid instructions like "10 pages maximum with 1.5 line spacing"
or "3 pages per capability section" standardize proposal formats for equitable
side-by-side comparisons.

Constrained responses also benefit bidders through added focus on differentiating capabilities most aligned to selection criteria rather than over-investing in
speculative periphery offerings. Restrictions demand prioritization crystallizing
true competitive advantages versus "nice to have" features that clutter distract
from core messages.

When facing tight space constraints:

Prioritize Core Strengths

Frame content directly addressing must-have RFP requirements and heavily weighted evaluation criteria matrix elements. Build messaging around clear value propositions derived from competitive capabilities, proven methodologies, and specialized expertise that compel selection.

Streamline Supporting Details

Pare down supplementary sections to summarize only essential supporting details like high-level implementation timelines, customer success briefs, or company background overviews. Relocate non-essential sections into appendices without guaranteed reviewer exposure.

Simplify Language

Use clear, concise phrasing to maximize information density within word limits. Eliminate verbose filler terms, boil down figures of speech, and avoid unnecessary repetition. Every word must serve a purpose.

Applying these principles crystallizes proposals around differentiated strengths matching client needs. Constraining responses filters out diversions from core messages that dilute persuasive arguments. A compelling case at the right length proves more powerful than an unfocused case with more pages.

How to Structure Your Bid

When structuring your RFP response, it's crucial to adhere to the client's instructions regarding content and organization, even if their requirements differ from your usual approach. In public sector procurement, RFPs typically outline the necessary elements of a submission, leaving little room for deviation. Failing to provide the requested information can result in the rejection of your bid.

In other contexts outside public sector procurement, you may have more flexibility in determining the content of your RFP response. Regardless of the situation, it's vital to remember that your bid serves the client's needs, not your own. There are several categories of information that clients typically expect to find in every RFP response:

Statement of Purpose and Bidder Identity: Begin by clearly stating the purpose of your bid and identifying the bidder(s).

Understanding of Client's Objectives: Demonstrate your appreciation of the client's objectives, showcasing your comprehension of the project's context, contract requirements, and the professional effort it entails.

Technical Approach and Methods: Provide an overview of your proposed technical approach and the methods you intend to employ.

Intended Outcomes and Deliverables: Clearly outline the expected outcomes of the project and the deliverables you will provide.

Work Plan and Timetable: Present a work plan with a detailed timetable, including a visual representation like a bar chart that illustrates the work program, timescales, and completion dates for each project phase.

Personnel Assignments: Specify the personnel assigned to the project, along with their competencies and individual responsibilities.

Management Arrangements and Performance Monitoring: Describe your management arrangements and procedures for monitoring project performance and delivery.

Policies and Procedures: Provide details of the policies and procedures you apply in relevant fields such as health and safety, equality and diversity, environmental management, and customer care.

Contractor Background and Experience: Highlight your background as a contractor, your qualifications for the assignment, and your experience in similar or related work.

Fees and Expenses: Include an estimate or confirmation of the fees and expenses expected to be incurred.

Beyond these minimum requirements, three additional elements can significantly enhance the effectiveness and competitiveness of your bid:

(i) **Summary:** Begin with a summary that outlines the key points of your proposal and emphasizes its value to the client.

(ii) **Response Matrix:** Create a response matrix that lists the requirements specified in the tender documents, as well as any additional matters raised by the client. Indicate where and how these points are addressed within your bid.

(iii) **Glossary or Quick Reference Index:** Consider including a glossary of technical terms or a quick reference index that lists topics discussed in the bid, relevant issues, items, and locations. Place this index ahead of the main text for easy reference.

Structure your RFP response into sections that align with the categories of information mentioned above. Additionally, be sure to accommodate any specific client requirements regarding project execution and management, such as sections on quality procedures or risk management.

While it may be tempting to include marketing brochures or other promotional materials, it's generally best to avoid them in your RFP response. Such materials can give the impression of attempting to inflate the bid or suggest that it's not custom-tailored for the specific contract. Clients often focus on the content directly related to the contract rather than general marketing materials. Instead, use a few paragraphs written specifically for the occasion to convey the value your services offer and how your skills and resources align with the client's objectives.

In the case of e-tendering procedures, introductory sections are typically omit-ted. However, when submitting a hard copy of your RFP response, it can be beneficial to include an initial section that identifies the invitation or opportu-nity to which you are responding. This section should outline the document's structure and content.

In the introductory section, quote the client's reference information and other relevant details. Mention the date and signatory if the tender is in response to a specific contract notice, letter, fax, or email. If it results from a different form of contact, provide an explanation of that interaction. Remember that the person evaluating the tender may not necessarily be the same individual who sent the invitation or signed the initial communication.

If you are collaborating with other contractors in a group or consortium, pro-vide information about each organization separately. Explain their respective roles and responsibilities within the contract and clarify what each partner contributes to the team's work. Specify the contracting party if the group is awarded the contract. Emphasize the cohesion and balance of the integrated group, highlighting its strengths and justifying its formation.

Consider including a matrix showcasing the team or contractor's relevant expe-rience. This matrix can highlight recent work for the client or related authorities, particularly in sectors of expertise related to the project. If any team members have a history of successful work with the client, make sure to highlight this as well. The matrix should appear comprehensive, demonstrating the relevance of each entry.

Technical Approach and Methodology

This section should outline how you will complete the project. The goal is showing that you understand what the client wants to achieve and that your methods will meet their needs. Be clear and detailed in explaining your step-by-step process.

First, restate the objectives and desired outcomes from the request for proposal (RFP). This shows you comprehend what the client is looking for. Next, describe the techniques and tasks you will use during each phase of the project. Explain how they directly connect to fulfilling the stated requirements. Break it down into simple bullet points for readability.

Back up your approach by summarizing comparable successful projects you've completed in the past. Quantify the methods you used and the concrete results achieved. This instills confidence that you can replicate success. It also indicates you have hands-on experience versus solely theoretical knowledge.

Specify what information, participation or assets you will require from the client to perform the work. This demonstrates you understand the working relationship. It also allows the client to assess the reasonableness of your expectations.

Lastly, address potential risks or changes that may arise if circumstances shift or assumptions do not hold. Present contingency plans and show adaptability in your solution. Reiterate that your methodology directly serves the objectives and requirements outlined at the beginning.

Using clear technical specifics grounded in past success convinces the client you grasp and can deliver on their needs. It positions your solution as both capable and reliable. Keep explanations simple and focused.

Resource Management

This section should introduce the qualified personnel who will work on the project. For each team member, explain:

- Their name and role

- Years of experience in this field

- Specific skills and credentials

- Past projects similar to this one

Breaking down each member's background shows you have the talent needed to succeed. It also assigns accountability for key tasks.

List your project manager first. Detail their tenure overseeing comparable contract work and highlight their successes delivering complex initiatives on budget and schedule. Then map their oversight of resources, schedules, compliance, quality control, and client communications. Most importantly, build them up for the client to put their trust in them.

Next list the day-to-day technical lead executing the work. Specify their hands-on experience aligning project tasks and methodologies to meet client requirements. Quantify their contribution to positive past outcomes. Detail their responsibility for technical design and implementation.

Finally, note supporting analysts, specialists, etc. that will develop assets, conduct research, compile data, and produce deliverables. Summarize their qualifications and assignment areas tied to distinct project phases.

Conclude by restating your commitment to open communication with the client. Underscore the team's blend of deep expertise, proven experience, and role clarity. This instills confidence you have the dedicated personnel and organization to deliver results. It also enables transparency and accountability over resources and outcomes.

Outcomes and Deliverables

This section connects promised project outcomes back to the request for proposal (RFP) requirements. It details what specific assets or results will be achieved at each stage. Clarity around expected deliverables provides accountability to scope.

Restate from the RFP the key objectives, technical specifications, and project timeline you will follow. This directly aligns to the client needs driving the initiative. Then break out deliverables into phases matching the timeline. For example:

Planning Stage

- Project plan detailing tasks, schedules, roles

- Analysis of current workflows vs. optimization goals

- Finalized success metrics

Execution Stage

- Solution prototype

- Mid-point status update on development progress

- Testing results measured against metrics

Completion Stage

Deliver the finished product/service, such as:

- New system functioning fully per technical specifications

- All data migrated and accessible

- Knowledge transfer sessions with client team

- Going live support during transition

Quantify what success looks like at every step, citing previous results where possible. This demonstrates you understand and can deliver on expectations. It also allows the client to monitor advancement toward clearly defined outcomes.

Plainly detailing what will be achieved when builds confidence you comprehend the end goals. Clients can clearly hold you accountable to schedule, budget and receiving what they purchased.

Present Your Price Estimates

This section should clearly detail the total proposed price, fee structure, and cost breakdowns tied back to delivering the request for proposal (RFP) scope. Competitive pricing requires aligning to budget expectations, communicating value, and demonstrating price integrity.

Start by restating the established RFP budget or client cost target stated in initial discussions. Position your total fixed pricing as hitting or beating this benchmark through process efficiencies or value pricing models. Break pricing down into understandable line items tied to project phases and deliverables. For example:

- Planning - $X (project management, workflows analysis, reporting dashboard setup)

- Execution - $Y (system prototype, development, content migration/integration)

- Completion - $Z (quality assurance testing, training, go-live transition support)

Support your pricing by summarizing the value delivered versus cost. Highlight areas you provide more services, higher SLAs, or better terms than typical market rates. Reference long-term cost savings or productivity gains your solution enables.

Lastly, describe the integrity behind your quoted pricing. Explain there are no hidden fees and all aspects of your services are represented transparently. Highlight that you operate on fixed pricing models versus billable hours. Underscore there will be no surprise rate hikes down the road.

Include Appendices

Appendices bolster the main proposal with documentation that validates capabilities without cluttering key messages. Use them strategically to showcase qualifications, share relevant work samples, and build credibility.

Possible appendix content includes:

- **Staff Credentials:** Attach condensed resumes demonstrating your team's expertise, certificates confirming qualifications, and licenses verifying legal approval to perform services.

- **Case Studies:** Share client case studies, project reports, technical specifications, and scientific whitepapers proving you have successfully executed on comparable initiatives.

- **Client Testimonials:** Include quotes and reviews from past clients detailing your services, work product quality, adherence to budgets/timelines, and ongoing support.

- **Company Background:** Provide an overview of your organization's history, capabilities, specialties, past performances, and quality standards certifications.

- **Signed Agreements:** Add letters of intent, formal subcontractor partnerships, account commitments from vendors/suppliers, and other legally executed documents that confirm allocated resources to fulfill contract obligations.

- **References:** Furnish a list of clients willing to discuss their firsthand experience working with you as well as your performance.

Innovation In Your Response

Rather than defaulting to a typical proposal outline, view unspecified formatting as a chance to showcase creativity. Customized organization can capture attention, yet execution must enhance versus obscure your qualifications. When applying an original framework:

Aligning with Industry Norms

When shaping an innovative structure, ensure overall organization still maps to established best practices. Completely unfamiliar patterns that diverge too extremely from norms can work against credibility even when content is robust. Reinforce strengths foremost.

For example, expectations exist across sectors that RFP responses lead with administrative compliance checklists, transition into company overviews, build into technical capability showcases, and close with pricing tables. Deviate mildly perhaps by moving cost ahead of qualifications. But take care not to push format radically outside sector comfort zones solely for novelty's sake at the expense of optics.

While some innovation demonstrates visionary thinking, dramatic departures risk implied unreliability. Keep customary scaffolds in place that lend dependability. Creativity should smooth versus sever ties to conventions expected from reputable providers. Use original elements to support versus supplant industry standards.

Centering Content Authority

When applying an innovative structure, technical expertise must lead. Format originality should never outweigh capability competencies as primary emphasis. While template patterns impact optics, strengths substance must headline.

For example, flashy visuals drawing interest toward innovative frameworks could inadvertently redirect focus from credential confirmation needed to evaluate qualifications. Lead unambiguously with expertise citing evidence of past performances, key talent acquirement, operational capacities, and project comprehensions that foreground abilities to deliver.

Dressings of ingenuity should drape versus disguise stalwarts of reliability. Content carries weight; decorum supports. Formulate responses to showcase competencies first, with creative elements only to bolster authority. Optimal frameworks put technical qualifications center stage while performance record gives form legitimacy in supporting role.

Retaining Accessibility

When modifying standard response structures, retain easy accessibility to required content areas. Information hiding, disjointed connections or obscured details that make critical evaluation difficult must be avoided. Streamline access despite sections shifting.

For example, pricing tables may migrate ahead of typical sequence, but remain clearly labeled and page-referenced in the roadmap. Project plans might be divided across methodology and delivery sections, but still comprehensive when reconstituted. Creative layouts should aid understanding, not complicate information tracking.

In essence, innovative organizing opens avenues without obstructing pathways to necessity. Style supports while substance sustains at the fore. Form enriches without inhibiting function. Client evaluators ultimately require details served to discern; serve content evidently amidst inventive shaping.

Furnishing a Format Roadmap

When applying an innovative structure, furnish a roadmap upfront that explicates purpose. Explain each segment, what details it encompasses, and how sections connect into a cohesive flow. Mapping aids navigation of new terrain.

Unfamiliar organization without guides risks disorientation. A roadmap eases passage by noting direction to destinations sought - be they technical specs in the capabilities segment, pricing tables under value modeling sections, etc. Wayfinding allows audiences to traverse formatted innovation with confidence by understanding where elements reside.

Signposted shaping also builds logic, upholding rationality when diverging from the routine. Reasons behind refreshed restraints come to light. Justify approaches as enhancements that support communication or demonstrations of technical alignment.

Developing Your RFP Response

Writing a bid that wins contracts balances showing experience with elevating client goals. Use practical observations, ideas aligned to objectives, transparent assumptions, and diplomatic clarifications to reinforce your fit. This builds trust in your expertise to fulfill expectations.

Demonstrating Relevant Experience

Showcase directly applicable experience executing similar contract work, such as:

- "Having implemented widget analytics systems for over 300 clients, we understand all essential integration, data migration and change management components needed to fulfill your program objectives."

- "Our team has configured variables testing for Fortune 500 ecommerce sites with over 5 million monthly visitors. We know critical considerations around balancing statistical significance with customer experience."

This proves you comprehend the practical realities of successful delivery while underscoring real-world qualifications.

Presenting Efficiency Ideas

Suggest methods that could enhance outcomes or processes without overstepping client ownership. For example:

- "From optimizing programs similar in scope, we've found greater cost efficiencies directing tier-1 work to specialized trained contractors while keeping strategic activities in-house."

- "When rapid prototype iteration is prioritized, we recommend two week deployment sprints to accelerate refinement versus monthly schedules."

This leverages experience to elevate their path to goals without overwriting existing plans. Naïvely challenging the client damages trust. Smart collaboration earns authority.

Noting Influential Elements

Detail where existing outlines have informed your approach, such as:

- "The success metrics defined on page 10 directly shaped our interim benchmarking targets explained in the project plan."

- "The geospatial and demographic data sets detailed on page 8 led us to select location-based targeting parameters for maximum cost efficiency."

This linkage signals customized fitting to needs versus recycled, generic solutions.

Stating Required Assumptions

Surface any reasonable assumptions made regarding undefined variables in client plans to preemptively align expectations, such as:

- "Given undefined timelines around required backend API upgrades, we've projected a Q3 release in our rollout schedule. Dates can be adjusted pending confirmation from your engineering team."

Transparency around need-to-know details prevents mismatched expectations while underscoring adaptation capabilities.

Clarifying Through Consultation

If client plans seem inadequate or contradictory, avoid overt critiques. Instead, suggest a collaborative clarification meeting:

- "To ensure we fully comprehend nuanced priorities around rigidity of rollout deadlines versus priorities around feature depth, we welcome a consultation to clarify flexible options."

This diplomatic approach allows redirection while letting them save face and retain ownership of the vision.

Presenting Alternative Perspectives

Where alternative approaches could deliver superior solutions, frame suggestions around benevolently advancing their agenda:

- "With deep expertise optimizing supply chain workflows, our team recognizes potential bottlenecks from lengthy staging processes. We believe we can deliver outcomes faster while cutting costs by reducing staging formalities as explained in our methodology."

This asserts your method as the surest way to achieve their vision while keeping the focus on their goals instead of your own convenience.

Discussion versus Demands

Rather than issuing top-down critiques or demands in response to unclear, inadequate or contradictory plans:

- Pose clarifying questions that allow clients to save face

- Recommend collaborative consultation sessions to explore alternatives

- Cite your experience seamlessly elevating past clients' outcomes

The approach should be consultative and one of partnership, rather than transactional.

Chapter Eight

Defining the Deliverables

There is an important difference between the outcomes a client wants to achieve from a contract and the concrete deliverables provided. Outcomes satisfy the strategic needs driving the project. For example, increased revenue, reduced costs, improved customer satisfaction, mitigated risks, enhanced workflows and other critical benefits prioritized by the client. Deliverables represent the tactical goods and services contractually pledged to the client per the agreement. This includes reports, plans, analysis, technology products, software deliverables, strategy guides, training sessions, and other work products produced.

While deliverables prove accountability through progress milestones, their core purpose is enabling outcomes so client goals are ultimately achieved. They actualize the strategic priorities and expected benefits behind the contract by reliably delivering results. Experienced clients recognize proposals that balance delivering immediate contractual obligations with understanding and optimizing long-term success metrics.

Winning bidders must therefore demonstrate practical mastery linking deliverables to outcomes in their response. For example, promising bi-weekly performance reports on a campaign (tactical deliverable) in order calibrate messaging to lift conversion rates by 15% (strategic outcome). This proves you grasp not just isolated output requirements but bigger picture needs to move key performance indicators. It spotlights dependable execution applied to progress external business priorities.

Top RFP responses express competency detailing specific deliverables plotted to reliably achieve communicated outcomes. You showcase technical capacities to complete contract work paired with insightful comprehension of client environments and priorities. This earns authority as a true strategic partner versus merely a vendor selling outputs.

Structuring Contract Deliverables

A clear schedule of deliverables enable clients to track contract progression while providing accountability milestones for your team. When shaping the project pace remember to:

Adhere to Client Plans

A clear deliverable schedule enables clients to track contract progression while providing accountability milestones for your team. When shaping project pace, established timelines around key decision checkpoints, activity completions, and work stages should be adhered to. Sync your team's cadence to specified rhythms or proactively suggest optimizations if predefined pace seems unrealistic to execute well.

Map Obligations

In situations without an explicit cadence, lay out a timeline meeting known expectations around delivering core contractual responsibilities. For example, detail routine progress reports submission, data analysis delivery, solution prototyping, training alignment stages etc.

You should plot completion points for all deliverables and work backwards from the finish line to ensure adequate cycles for constructing each foundational layer skillfully so final review and approval deadlines remain achievable.

Plot Completion Points

The completion deliverable allowing client signoff could involve presenting a summarizing report that codifies key learnings, decisions and next steps from the engagement.

Alternatively, hosting an explanatory session to leadership teams sharing synthesized findings. Or facilitating a collaborative workshop debating implementation implications. Flag any assumptions around unspecified completion criteria to preemptively realign visions.

Delivering End Goals

While management documentation represents consistent obligations across contracts, deliverable types also vary widely by sector. From software products, analytical models, design blueprints, training curriculum, campaign assets and more - diverse output actualizes desired ends. Their integrated harmony signals contract success.

Mapping milestones through finish demonstrates dependability. Reasoned pacing conveys care and capability while underscoring what completeness requires. Deliverable diversity details may differ but discipline in orchestrating interwoven elements inspires confidence in the conductor.

Management Documentation

Reports frame progress, codify learnings, and archive accomplishments. Strategic documentation lends vision, grounds teams, and prepares next stages.

Tracking Project Advancement

Progress reports provide interval check-ins, such as:

Monthly Recaps - Digest key accomplishments, decisions, or adjustments over the past month to affirm alignment.

Quarterly Previews - Detail major initiatives targeted for the upcoming quarter to focus efforts and resources.

Tie frequency to contract rhythms like review meetings or audit schedules. Tailor distribution method to client preferences whether online interfaces, digital files, or hard copies.

Inception Reports

Inception reports finalize contract specifics after initial ramp-up by:

- Reconfirming project assumptions

- Detailing adjusted timelines

- Identifying additional data inputs

- Codifying milestones

This grounds teams in realities taking shape during activation before inertia settles.

Completion and Final Reports

Completion reports archive key developments, learnings and outcomes. Incorporate:

- An executive overview of major milestones

- Recaps of pivotal challenges and solutions

- Budget utilization analysis

- Next phase recommendations

Comprehensive archives memorialize accomplishments to date and prepare for what lies ahead.

Technical Documentation

Technical documents require balance - translating complexities without losing comprehension or distorting integrity. Strategic deliverables educate audiences while archiving processes for posterity.

Constructing Project Foundations

Before promising extensive technical memorandums, gauge client needs, project unknowns, and audience gaps warranting elaboration. Avoid overextending capacity. Instead suggest:

- Jointly identifying knowledge gaps with the greatest impact

- Prioritizing 1-3 memorandums around pivotal analyses optimizing outcomes

- Reviewing integration viability beyond concise reporting

This demonstrates discernment. It pivots from product push to partnership prioritization.

Plotting Informational Waypoints

Interim reports update progress, reveal preliminary insights, and frame downstream directions at critical milestones such as:

- Stage completions indicating viable paths forward

- Decision junctions requiring selection between options

- Validation checkpoints confirming solution integrity

They enable mid-course adjustments while memorializing pivotal precedents.

Archiving Comprehensive Discoveries

Final reports demand extensive yet consumable detail. Best practices include:

- Submitting initial drafts for internal stakeholder review

- Incorporating substantive feedback before external release

- Codifying complex data into executive summaries for simplified sharing

This allows secrecy-sensitive vetting while extending reach to educate leadership.

Humanizing Complex Concepts

For public dissemination, craft consultation summaries conveying complex concepts in accessible language. Relatable explanations bring non-technical stakeholders into the conversation to enrich impact.

The most convincing deliverables balance detail with clarity, enable ownership while educating, and serve posterity by documenting milestones masters can learn from.

Regular Project Documentation Reports

Set aligned expectations around report formatting including:

Medium Requests: Confirm quantity of hard copies needed plus specifications on electronic document files whether PDF, Word, Excel etc.

Software Standards: Record the client's operating environment including preferred platforms, operating systems and software compatibility needs to ensure accessible end products.

Rights and Usage: Define who retains ownership and publication rights over report contents - you as the independent expert or the client as underwriting organization. Allow for reviews ensuring internal stakeholder alignment.

Adhering to client preferences and standards signals responsiveness. It conveys you listen then deliver. But more than mere checkboxing, alignment eases usage which enables application. The more actionable the outputs, the more effective your solution becomes. Consider format a dimension of function.

Setting high standards for published work products motivate excellence. With public scrutiny or leadership visibility, teams intuit a mandate to craft exceptionally thoughtful, water-tight arguments in their project reports and documentation, able to withstand critique. The audience expands from a manager to a jury as they raise benchmarks by bringing reports to life as decision-making tools versus merely administrative artifacts filed upon submission. This drives clarity, creativity and care - elevating your counsel while earning authority.

Chapter Nine

Selling Value With Your Bid

T o make their bids successful, companies must go further than simply citing basic technical skills or histories. Providing exceptional value that unites futuristic thinking with clear benefits surpasses minimal submissions.

While others can match core abilities, you distinguish yourself with understandings they do not possess.

Notice unspoken wants, place distinctive assets in measurable terms, and convey thorough knowledge of how your tailored approach singularly propels goals. This level of value-added insight is what attracts contracts; Spotlighting novel solutions combined with full grasp of a client's aims shows how you will give them an edge. Your submission should go beyond the ordinary to prove your competitive advantage, securing the work through a vision of value other bidder cannot portray.

Decoding Desired Value

Rather than assumptions, deductively gather signals within specifications around prioritized areas for adding value. Some RFPs state this explicitly. Often reading between lines and understanding wider business contexts implies key gaps to fill. Pinpoint then deliver on unmet wants.

Four core value types to address include:

Financial - Efficiency gains, revenue generation, budget optimization, risk management. These impact the bottom line.

Strategic - Fulfilling goals around innovation, change management, economic growth. These progress vision.

Capacity - Improving outputs, strengthening competencies, increasing responsiveness. These elevate operations.

Relational - Exceeding expectations, sharing best practices, pushing boundaries. These emphasize partnership.

Targeting Priorities

With insight into which dimensions hold weight, respond decisively. For example:

If seeking financial value - Quantify how your solution saves money or creates opportunity.

If strategic value - Connect your approach directly to their goals.

If capacity value - Show how you amplify abilities and output.

If relational value - Demonstrate commitment to their success.

Back claims with facts - data, case evidence, expert testimony. This proves superiority.

Sustaining Perceived Worth

Value must align with client contexts versus assumptions. Frame it around their priorities backed by proof it delivers. This perceived worth sustains past the sales pitch through application. Position your solution as precisely right for them specifically.

Ongoing engagements also allow new internal advocates to experience benefits firsthand. Continually re-sell by asking strategic questions that reframe perspectives and propel continuous improvements. Clients ultimately cement value judgments, so perpetually over-deliver.

Standing Out From the Crowd

With competencies held equal amongst contenders, emphasize unmatched dimensions targeting client priorities to position unrivaled fit. Comb through specifications to uncover niche insights competitors lack. Fill explicit gaps and implied needs with precision to show mastery others miss.

Make their success your purpose. This level of value cannot be copied or bought because it stems from unique comprehension of their challenges and contexts. Stand out by doubling down on dimensions they deem most valuable both now and through delivery.

Protecting the Shared Interests

While technical qualifications inspire, risk protections build durable trust in partnerships primed for mutual success.

Particularly for important engagements, contractors would be wise to emphasize the safeguards they provide against uncertainty. Clearly laying out contingencies, backup provisions and risk mitigation plans assuages client concerns about unforeseen complications. It signals the supplier's commitment to the well-being of the partnership, not just project completion. Ensuring mutual protection of interests through carefully managed vulnerabilities and insulated downside exposure gives clients faith the supplier views this as a true alliance, not merely a transaction.

This enduring trust is built when suppliers make evident their comprehensive approach for how challenges will be weathered together. Outlining precautions translates technical capacity into reliable, interdependent progress resilient to difficulties. It provides reassurance to choose a counterpart dedicated to the shared prosperity of both parties through unity in overcoming risks.

Preparing for Turbulence

Whether situations, assumptions, or ambiguous variables - enumerate exposures inherent to the engagement scope. Bringing such exposures to light allows for subsequent contingency action-planning should conditions take a turn for the worse. Pre-emptively addressing potential threats in this manner demonstrates foresight, rather than later facing accusations of being unready or unrealistic.

Enumerating variables that could impact progress on the project prepares both parties to safeguard interests through alternative approaches if unforseen circumstances arises. Suppliers show prudence by surface level exposures at the outset so robust contingency measures may be strategized collaboratively to prevent downturns from hindering objectives. This upfront evaluation of ambiguities and assumptions fosters resilience when situations evolve beyond expectations.

Detailing Defenses

For each risk named, detail robust response plans that shield outcomes and relationships:

- Temporary resource allocators to absorb workflow fluctuations

- Proven templates ensuring repeatable processes amid disruption

- Reserves and buffers provisioned for contingency deployment

- Monitoring protocols flagging severity spikes before critical

This underscores preparation to maintain service levels if exogenous shocks require adaptation.

Embodying Collective Care

More than bulletproofing operations alone, convey shared vigilance ensuring both client and provider sustain. Express in tone and plans that interests indelibly intertwine - their resilience enables your performance.

Detail oversight procedures, status touchpoints, and transparent data flows embedding collaboration into the very fabric of delivery. Success rests on unified vulnerability management, so promote persists through unified vision guarding shared potential.

With confident, preventative posture, threats recede as possibilities grow. Protect by preparing, unite by caring - forging durable bonds where each party enables the other.

Building an All-Star Team

Highly competitive bids assemble dedicated experts from various specializations who are joined by a unified motivation to advance the client's goals.

By introducing these specialists and exhibiting how their diverse talents align to form a cohesive team, suppliers illustrate the depth and breadth of their abilities. Profiles of individuals comprising the proposed project group reinforce the supplier's competence while humanizing their qualifications. Readers envision real partnerships taking shape to power the initiative.

This customized assembly of all-stars instills confidence the supplier comprehends requirements at a granular level and can bring appropriate expertise to seamlessly address any concern. Suppliers allow clients to meet proposed team members and see for themselves the integrated strengths that will elevate performance. Showcasing team cohesion in this way underscores a supplier's preparedness to make the client's vision attainable through united excellence.

Cultivating Collective Character

Rather than isolated experts, detail a strategically formulated ensemble to attack specific challenges. For example:

A visionary strategist charting the course through uncertainty. An eagle-eyed data miner revealing insights that reframe perspectives. A nimble collaborator harnessing strengths across boundaries.

Distil archetypical attributes that propel progress then locate exemplars who embody them. This moves beyond basic qualifications checks toward purposeful personality prioritization.

Communicate Cohesion

Illustrate how varied strengths fuse into a cohesive unit that nimbly navigates projects needs. For example:

The strategist scans macro environments to identify influence shifts that could bolster or threaten the client business. The data miner translates numbers into narratives explaining how past decisions shaped current realities. The linker connects their outputs into recommendations refine objectives and tactics.

This interconnected leverage multiplies the team's collective impact beyond the sum of individual contributions.

Embodying Your Ethos

Ultimately your crew symbolizes your organization's character and abilities much as all-star players represent their sport's highest levels.

Whether marshalling cross-department diplomats, subject matter iconoclasts, creative sparks or execution athletes, the assembled ensemble broadcasts your competence to handle complex assignments.

Their harmony sings of capacities to deliver results by combining exactly the right people. And culture resounds - who you select signals what you value. Their composition becomes your identity.

Operationalizing Your Competitive Advantages

To set proposals apart, suppliers must illustrate how dedicated procedures and specialized tools used in their operations would distinctly optimize outcomes, productivity, and one-upmanship for this client's needs.

By detailing inventive methods and systems designed specifically with the engagement's priorities in mind, companies exemplify their forward-thinking approach versus a standardized replication of past work. A submission enlightening clients on innovations planned for seamlessly handling their requirements positions the supplier as a pioneer, not just an emulator of others. Such unique optimization techniques and purpose-built technologies become valuable competitive differentiators when suppliers effectively communicate results clients can foreseeably obtain.

Operationalizing advantages through insights shared elevates the perceptions of your strategic abilities to surpass expectations profitably with their customized operational prowess.

Streamlining Outcomes

Methods should be detailed that strengthen results. For example, explain a Six Sigma-certified business analysis framework that identifies root causes behind output defects using statistical models, yielding a 30% improved quality ratings. Claims must be supported with quantified past impacts across varied client contexts by providing case studies or success stories of happy clients. This makes proposed advantages concrete rather than theoretical.

Optimizing Efficiencies

Analytical tools, predictive models or automated techniques that accelerate workflows or reduce costs should be described. For instance, explain a machine learning platform that forecasts increases in contract objections 48 hours before they occur, enabling mitigation efforts that have minimized disputes by 22%. The benefits of systems must be backed by pilot findings on similar projects. Specific details sell credibility.

Future-Proofing Operations

New leading-edge systems designed to ready clients for coming changes should be explained. As an example, describe a blockchain initiative modernizing supply chain traceability to meet emerging regulatory compliance needs such as requirements X, Y and Z. While perhaps unusual now, demonstrate how bold investments will crystalize a forward-looking system. Although counterintuitive, showing how clients gain competitive advantages through proactive compliance is key.

Overall, proposed advantages come to life through case-specific context, quantified results and a future orientation beyond today's standard technologies and business practices. Evidence and foresight build confidence in partnership proposals.

Share ventures that manifests your vision despite them not being industry convention yet. Whether maximizing present progress or pioneering prospective tools, position yourself as both actualizing achiever and innovator. Pair concrete examples of your past performance with potential of future develops and capabilities to widen the competitive distance between yourself and others.

Distinct processes signify distinct outcomes...and distinctions capture contracts.

Promising and Providing Value

Successful proposals go further than merely meeting basic expectations.

Innovative concepts that exceed requirements and provide unexpected benefits showcase thorough insight into the client's underlying aims. Suggesting inventive solutions indicates forethought into what truly drives their objectives rather than a limited view of surface needs. Suppliers demonstrate their role as an advocate empowering the realization of aspirations, not merely as an ordinary service provider. Promising illuminating value that stimulates and satisfies unseen wants establishes yourself as a visionary partner.

Through proposing ingenious strategies aligned with the spirit of the client's vision, not just contract specifics, suppliers set themselves apart as invested champions of driving progress - not just transactional vendors fulfilling tasks. This positioning nurtures loyalty by proving comprehensive support for propelling what matters most to the client's goals.

Accelerating Returns on Investment

Propose supplementary initiatives that optimize client outcomes, such as:

- An immediate quick-win workshop targeting high-potential gaps revealed during discovery that swiftly boosts performance.

- Contextualized training programs upskilling staff on pivotal competencies needed to sustain solution impact over time.

- Temporary specialist secondments mentoring internal teams on vital replication protocols during transition windows.

This obligates while impressing. Drive their success further through your unrequired efforts to enable adoption.

Magnifying Reach

Suggest additional output vehicles that broaden solution impact, such as:

- Project newsletters broadcasting updates to wider audiences.

- Public web pages explaining key features for external community education.

- Archived evergreen best practice content as an ongoing technical resource.

This expands your deliverable's influence beyond intended users to peripheral stakeholders.

Ultimately, promising more cements perception of your solution as an investment versus a transaction. Your success ties to theirs, so you strive to ensure outcomes endure. This emotional connection fosters partnership beyond the project.

Surpass checklist expectations by caring then contributing beyond contract requirements in ways that empower their organization specifically. This earns affinity along with authority.

Renewing Engagements Through Continuous Value

To sustain successful partnerships beyond initial contracts, suppliers must cultivate lasting value founded on strong bonds, unique understandings and dependability.

Renewing proposals revisit former successes together with a strategic analysis of how vulnerabilities were fortified to become strengths. Revisiting milestones achieved renews the client's confidence while thoughtfully inspecting prior exposures indicates a supplier's commitment to longevity through diligence.

Suppliers entrench their place as a long-term strategic resource by signifying relevance to changing circumstances through progressive relationships, fresh perspectives and proven reliability under renewed risks. Reaffirming one's position as an integral ally requires transparently re-experiencing journeys walked side by side and envisioning next steps from an posture of knowledge and care for the client's evolving needs.

This ongoing nurturing of an indispensable, forward-thinking role is what ensures premier suppliers remain favored advisors for the life of fruitful partnerships.

Leveraging Institutional Knowledge

Having completed previous work, detail unique interfaces granting insider perspectives competitors lack, such as:

- Nuances around internal decision-maker tensions requiring navigation

- Proficiency with proprietary systems and datasets

- Contextual awareness guiding communications for alignment

This demonstrates key learning only longevity enables. Familiarity signals reduced disruptions, risks, and ramp-up needs given established rapport and knowledge.

Revisiting Shortcomings

If past projects exposed weaknesses, preemptively acknowledge and address them by:

- Explaining the breakdowns and specifics improvements to prevent recurrence.

- Outlining additional controls and measures now in place across operations elevating standards.

- Reviewing lessons learned and formalized changes to underscore growth versus stagnation.

This transparency regarding past performance paired with demonstrable Evolution encourages re-engagement based on new advantages.

Relating Through Progress

At their heart, proposals must convey a team's dedication to prosperity gained in unison through steady premium efforts and benefits fostered. Examples demonstrating a supplier's work enhancing a client's competence, empowering management with visionary perspectives, or quickening strides toward pivotal aims personalize collaborative partnerships over singular deals. Stories showcasing how a supplier's assistance strengthened clients' positions frames a team as invested allies, not removed vendors.

Sharing clear instances of clients excelling to new altitudes hand-in-hand crafts a compelling narrative of a supplier committed to carrying and being carried by their clients as fellow travelers on the journey upward. Relatable snapshots illuminating clients empowered by the team's assistance to achieve more cement pursuits as conjoined rather than solitary. This framing nurtures confidence in selecting a supplier capable of, and passionate about, elevating performance through progressive cooperation over disconnected transactions alone defined by fleeting targets met.

Staying Ahead of Alternatives

To continuously distinguish one's value proposition, proposals must convey adeptness combined with advancement. Position these new dimensions that widen your capabilities gap versus substitutes and compeition. Introduce innovations like:

- Proprietary techniques honed through recent field work refining efficiency

- Complimentary services enlarged by new specialized talent partnerships

- Agile project management methods created in alignment with their shifting preferences

Suppliers retain their competitive advantage by displaying versatile skills refined over time as well as a commitment toward innovations yet unseen by others.

Exhibiting expansive potential for growth alongside steadiness instills confidence in long-term leadership. Examples highlighting new capacities branching from core strengths fortify relevance in changing climates by progressing what is proven while probing what may prove. Concurrently, ease cultivated from comfort in responsibilities performed solidifies reliance during interruptions. Together, this flexibility and the foundations you've built will form a dual assurance of able direction under uncertainties of teh future.

Suppliers survive cuts by balancing mature prowess with motivations inspiring destinations beyond present vistas. This packaging of adaptable alacrity next to seasoned surety maintains distances from trailing imitators over enduring roadways.

Chapter Ten

Validating Capabilities

R FPs represent major business opportunities, but winning them requires suppliers to convince prospective clients they can satisfy all requirements and deliver exemplary results. Hence RFP responses must validate bidding organizations' capabilities beyond any doubt through relevant evidence and linkage of past performance to future value. This is enabled by client references, descriptive case studies, and clearly articulating how previous experience will pragmatically resolve the client's needs.

The rationale behind requiring client references as part of RFP responses is to enable prospective customers to discover first-hand accounts of suppliers' competence and working relationships. References serve as credible external validators who can vouch for contractors' ability to not just execute the stated work, but also collaborate smoothly, adapt to unexpected changes, and create further value via innovation. Case studies further bolster such claims by richly detailing projects similar to the current tender with metrics quantifying success in alignment with client goals. They demonstrate domain expertise, evidence practical methodologies and tools applied to accomplish defined objectives within constraints.

However, merely providing summaries and tables of past assignments is insufficient for winning bids. Suppliers must compellingly highlight how positive outcomes and learnings will translate to addressing the new client's specific problems and opportunities. The narrative needs to identify parallels between previous challenges overcome and present scenarios, while also acknowledging differences that may require alternative approaches. By explaining proven techniques to handle related issues successfully, suppliers instill confidence in their understanding of core RFP requirements. This further strengthens the client's perception of contractors' vision and capability to achieve desired results. Hence combining credentials with an insightful linkage between experience and expected performance is key to validating overall value and tilt selections in one's favor.

Client References

Many request for proposals require suppliers to furnish contact details of previous clients who can vouch for their work quality and service delivery. This allows prospective customers to better evaluate suppliers' fit and competence for the tendered contract. Hence, responding accurately and transparently to such requirements is imperative.

Given that references enable assessing real-world performance, failing to provide adequate client contacts signals inability to prove one's experience. Since the very eligibility to bid depends on having requisite credentials, suppliers must furnish complete, valid references without hesitation. Vague, incomplete details that impede reference checks must be avoided. Prospective clients do contact references to evaluate capabilities.

Information to Provide

The specific identities and addresses of responsible client representatives must be shared to facilitate seamless communication. These individuals should have directly engaged the supplier earlier for comparably complex assignments. If available, include client sites where implemented solutions can be inspected. Essentially, comply fully and transparently with all reference requirements.

Client references validate expertise essential for contract awards. Hence suppliers must provide accurate, comprehensive contact information without opacity or omissions. Transparently proving capabilities builds trust and strengthens proposals.

Case Studies and Past Project Summaries

When bidding for contracts, suppliers must validate their ability to successfully deliver the work outlined in the RFP. A standard requirement is furnishing details of previous comparable projects through summaries and case studies. These demonstrate competence by highlighting relevant experience. However, certain best practices must be followed to ensure they adequately prove qualifications.

Ensuring Relevance

The projects cited should be relevant to the exact skills needed for the RFP's scope of work. The experience must also be recent, ideally from the past 5 years, since the expertise still resides with the bidder's current personnel. Additionally, the client representatives responsible for each cited contract should be named to facilitate reference checks. Any irrelevant, outdated or vague project descriptions will fail to validate capabilities.

Presenting a Judicious Selection

Some suppliers overwhelm prospective clients with excessive details spanning dozens of pages. However, it is advisable to concisely showcase a careful selection of about 5-10 highly relevant past projects, with summaries limited to 15-20 lines each. These should clearly describe the work's scope and objectives, methodology used, outputs delivered, team members involved, challenges overcome, and success achieving client goals within constraints. Avoid unnecessary verbiage that burdens the reader.

Emphasizing Management Capabilities

Technical expertise alone does not guarantee satisfactory delivery. Hence project summaries must also highlight managerial experience - the ability to marshal resources efficiently, coordinate collaborators, oversee complex assignments, and ultimately deliver per the client's expectations within budget and on schedule. Quantify such managerial success factors from past work where possible.

Adapting Content Sensitively

While most government and corporate clients freely feature as references, some request confidentiality regarding their engagement. Summaries of projects performed for such clients can exclude identifying details but still communicate the nature, methods and positive results of the work through generic descriptions like "a European telecommunications company," etc. Adapting content thus caters to clients' comfort levels.

Updating for Accuracy

Project records must be continually updated rather than presenting outdated summaries from when the work was still ongoing. So in project databases, new contracts should be logged from the outset, key documents archived on completion, and summaries promptly updated to reflect final deliverables, performance metrics, and measured impact. Maintaining accuracy is vital for the references to sustain credibility.

Project summaries and case studies must relevance, recency and accuracy to convincingly showcase suppliers' fit and qualification for proposed contracts. Following best practices to provide judicious and transparent evidence of positive past performance helps establish trust and competitive advantage.

Translating Past Performance into Future Value

When applying for new projects, it's important for companies to do more than just provide a basic list of past work. Listing previous jobs alone does not fully show how a company will use its experience to help future clients. Saying "we've done this before" is not enough.

Companies need to demonstrate a deeper understanding of what customers require and how their knowledge can specifically address new needs. To be successful in requests for proposals, suppliers must illustrate that they comprehend what the client wants to achieve. They should also explain how their skills and background learning from similar work positions them well to solve the problems involved in the upcoming project. Simply reporting on past performance does not communicate the relevance of a company's qualifications to potential new clients. A successful proposal shows understanding and application of expertise tempered with experience.

Core Components

An impactful RFP response integrates two components:

1. Summaries of comparable past work: Details like contract scope, methods used, outputs delivered, metrics of success, client references, etc. showcase credentials.

2. Narrative linkage to proposed work: This explains how previous experience produced positive outcomes, overcame comparable difficulties, and will now enable suppliers to pragmatically fulfill objectives for the new client.

Key Issues and Activities

Suppliers should identify key issues and critical activities needed to meet contract requirements based on their understanding. The relevance of experience is then established by giving examples of successfully handling similar issues and activities in the past.

The discussion should also address any expected differences between past work and the new project. Suppliers should clarify how learning from prior experience makes them ready to adjust accordingly. By detailing specific important issues, activities, and past examples of handling similar situations, a company shows the value of its qualifications. It also conveys its ability to transfer relevant knowledge and adapt its approach when needed. This establishes confidence that a supplier can rise to meet both the known and unknown challenges of the prospective work.

Illustrative Example

Consider an RFP to implement a customer data analytics platform. Summaries will first detail past systems integration, data migration and analytics configuration projects. Building on that, the narrative then explains how challenges like establishing data pipelines, validating reporting, and training employees were resolved through specific methods to improve operations in other organizations. It subsequently highlights how these proven techniques will be tailored to deliver an optimal solution for the prospective client in alignment with their environment and objectives.

RFP responses should not just tabulate experience but vividly demonstrate its applicability.

To truly convince potential clients, suppliers must vividly illustrate how their experience applies to the new work. Combining verifiable records of relevant achievements with a persuasive analysis of what was learned fosters belief that the company completely understands the client's requirements. Weaving together qualifications and a meaningful discussion of how those past successes inform the supplier's approach shows clients the supplier has tangible experience that can be effectively applied. This compelling portrayal assures clients the supplier will leverage practical lessons from similar work to deliver exceptional results under the new contract.

Through compellingly linking relevant project history with a discussion of significance, suppliers demonstrate for clients they are well-positioned through demonstrated experience to transform comprehension into exemplary performance.

Chapter Eleven

Presenting Financial Information

W hen providing pricing information in an RFP response, you must balance presenting a competitive bid to win the business with submitting a realistic quote you can deliver on. This section offers tips on including the pricing details clients request while positioning your organization as affordable yet able to meet project requirements.

Follow the instructions precisely for supplying pricing data like tables, forms, and additional financial verification documents. Carefully adhering to these guidelines allows for clear comparisons across bidders. Tailor any supplemental information like financial statements to underscore your stability and capability to take on the work.

Emphasize the value your solution delivers, not just the total cost. Break down pricing to showcase what is included with clear descriptions. Demonstrate you understand and can provide the specific quality of services the client seeks at a fair price.

Offer different pricing options the client can select from to match needs and budgets. This presents you as flexible and interested in finding the best fit versus maximizing profit. Outline any opportunities to adjust scope or timelines to further reduce costs.

RFP pricing often represents the final hurdle between being in the running versus getting eliminated. Providing competitive pricing following all instructions while highlighting the value you offer positions your organization as the affordable and capable choice. With an eye on budget along with solution quality and fit, you prove capable of delivering the "right price at the right quality" services clients require.

Pricing Information Breakdown

Clients want a clear picture of what factors make up your pricing to assess overall value for money. Providing a detailed cost breakdown builds trust and confidence that you have priced thoughtfully. This allows clients to better compare bids.

Follow all instructions around pricing formats like tables, forms, or schedules. Break pricing down into sections like stages, activities, deliverables, and expense categories. Show calculations and assumptions behind cost estimates.

List hourly or daily rates for team members along with estimated time involvement. Include a multiplier percentage to account for overheads if suitable. Outline travel, materials, or licensing expenses likely to arise.

Note any fixed prices tied to certain agreed deliverables or project milestones. Where appropriate, indicate costs anticipated at different points over the project timeline.

Offer tiered pricing structures or bulk discounts on multiple engagements. Clients want to understand opportunities to reduce costs through flexibility or combined work. Demonstrate openness to adjusting scope, timing, or staffing to control pricing.

Detailed pricing breakdowns may require more upfront effort but pay dividends in boosting your competitiveness and positioning you as a partner invested in the client's needs. Transparently showing how you arrive at project costs helps demonstrate thoughtfulness and reasonableness alongside overall value delivered.

Total Bid Price

State the total bid price prominently in both words and figures to prevent confusion. Note exactly what services the pricing covers by referencing the RFP's scope of work. Specify the applicable currency and tax treatment. Consider applying a modest contingency percentage to the total if the contract duration exceeds your projected delivery schedule. This cushions against unexpected changes in requirements or external factors.

However, do not pad pricing across the board as savvy clients will expect discounts on any conventional work unlikely to incur exceptional risk. If your bids are noticeably higher than competitors just to build in extra margin, clients may not trust that you understand their needs and budget. Save any premium pricing only for unique, complex projects that genuinely involve higher risks or specialized skills.

When evaluating RFP responses, clients will be watching closely to see which vendors demonstrate a realistic approach. Padding standardized work will make your bids seem inflated or unrealistic. It risks clients perceiving you don't respect their budget constraints. They may then award the work to competitors with more transparent, competitive bids for standard services.

Breakdown of Costs

Provide a detailed breakdown of what comprises the total bid price. Outline the estimated costs of each stage, phase, deliverable, and activity. Show calculations and assumptions. This granularity allows clients to understand value distribution and identify potential adjustment opportunities.

Follow any structural requirements in the RFP for presenting pricing information like tables, schedules, or forms. Common components to cover include:

- Hourly, daily, or monthly rates for personnel involved, grouped appropriately

- Estimated time allocation across resources

- Multiplier percentage to cover overhead and profit

- Itemized expenses likely to be incurred

- Allowances for travel and subsistence

Person Rates and Time Estimates

Provide a clear explanation of any rates presented for team members. Break these down to show gross salary, bonuses, benefits, insurance, leave and other components that factor into payroll costs. Indicate the assumed profit margin and overhead recovery percentages built into multipliers.

For time-based pricing, give detailed estimates of hours anticipated for different tasks or phases, tied to rates for relevant staff. Explain assumptions behind duration estimates based on experience with similar projects.

Expenses

Itemize project-related expenses likely to arise, grouped into common categories like travel, materials, licensing, communications, etc. Estimate amounts for each, noting typical allowances or limits imposed by public sector clients. Specify assumption that expenses will be reimbursed at cost with proofs of payment.

Consider providing tiered options around expense categories the client can select from to control these costs.

Cost Assumptions

Document any assumptions or decisions made in calculating pricing not expressly defined in the RFP:

- Period for which bid pricing remains valid

- Baseline date for cost estimates

- Index linking to allow for inflation

- Definitions of work day, week, month durations

- Applicable taxes and duties

- Client inputs expected

- Subcontracting arrangements

- Computing requirements

- Treatment of travel expenses

Critically, explain the assumed contract start date underlying pricing and the implications of material delays beyond a defined threshold duration.

For overseas contracts, covered additional assumptions like applicable currencies, exchange rates, tax liabilities, counterpart staffing, training provision and languages used.

Emphasize the need for the eventual contract to recognize inflation risks and include protections should costs escalate materially relative to bid pricing.

Detailed pricing breakdowns require substantial upfront effort however deliver material dividends in boosting bid competitiveness. They demonstrate thoughtfulness and transparency around how total cost derives from individual components. This evidence of pricing rigor and reasonableness builds client trust that you understand requirements and can deliver within budget. Thus, comprehensive yet flexible pricing information serves as a key pillar underpinning a compelling RFP response.

Structuring Payment Milestones

Defining appropriate payment terms, schedules, and conditions in your RFP response sets clear expectations around cash flow and getting paid for work delivered. This section offers tips on presenting payment details that balance protecting your business interests with accommodating client limitations.

Payment Schedule Alignment

Review payment provisions outlined in the RFP and align your response to these. For fixed-price contracts, base payments on approval of key deliverables or achievement of project milestones. For time and materials arrangements, structure invoices to the frequency requested like monthly.

If the RFP does not define payment details, propose schedules tailored to contract duration and cash flow requirements. Offer options the client can elect based on internal constraints – for example monthly, quarterly or milestone-linked payments.

Advance Payments

To ease initial outlays for materials, equipment or setup costs, consider requesting a modest advance payment such as 15% of total fees. Avoid specifying overly generous advances in your response however, as public sector clients generally resist accommodating these.

Note that you expect any advances would require a corresponding payment security guarantee arranged via bank or export credit agency. Emphasize your willingness to work with procurer preferences and constraints on this aspect.

Late and Non-Payers

Guard against the risk of late payments by having formal engagement letters signed before commencing work. Include clear payment due dates and state expected charges for undisputed late payments.

For new clients or smaller businesses where payment risk seems elevated, require 50% of fees as an advance payment. Explain this helps avoid misunderstandings down the line if organizations unfortunately face insolvency issues later on.

Having appropriate paperwork and advances in place also signals professionalism and reassures clients who readily appreciate the importance of agreed payment schedules.

Other Considerations

Accommodate client payment processing limitations due to periods for reviews, bureaucratic approvals etc by structuring payment timelines accordingly. Consider stretching out early progress payments if needed to ease their cash flow burdens.

Demonstrate flexibility around discussing payment terms during negotiations to balance both parties' business requirements. However, avoid leaving payment provisions entirely open-ended in your RFP response.

Thoughtfully aligning payment arrangements with client expectations while securing your business interests establishes trust and confidence in your services. Signaling readiness to structure payment timelines keyed to contract milestones and constraints further positions you as a flexible partner attuned to procurer needs and limitations.

Aim for Competitive yet Realistic Pricing

Pricing represents one of the most critical elements clients evaluate when reviewing RFP responses. Submitting a bid with unrealistic, inaccurate pricing risks losing out, while pricing too low creates delivery challenges that undermine project success and relationships. This article shares tips on developing pricing that balances competitiveness with achievability.

Streamlined Presentation

Keep pricing details focused only on essentials aligned to what the RFP requests. Avoid vague, catch-all categories like "admin expenses" unless the RFP specifically includes these. Check tables and figures match across sections where costs get presented at both summary and detailed levels.

Follow all RFP instructions meticulously around prescribed formats for presenting pricing information. Do not let standard internal cost schedules tempt you away from following provided templates. Even if requiring adaptation, diligent adherence signals responsiveness.

Review pricing thoroughly to confirm no inadvertent omissions or double counting. Any lack of clarity or inconsistencies around financial terms can undermine perceptions of bid quality.

Pricing Rigor and Flexibility

Develop pricing iteratively in tandem with refining technical approach. Treat costing with equal priority to avoid disconnects between price proposed and work needed to deliver per requirements.

Leverage spreadsheets to model different pricing scenarios balancing cost levers like:

- Team composition

- Time inputs

- Charge rates

- Expense allowances

This analysis spotlights whether RFP budgets adequately fit desired outcomes and where flexibility exists for negotiations.

If the work represents well-established offerings sold across clients, base pricing on average historical rates demonstrating subject matter expertise. For bespoke projects, develop pricing bottom-up tied to specific bid.

Broadly, aim to price competitively based on a target margin over forecasted costs. But given depressed market conditions or deal-specific constraints, be willing to compress margins to vie more effectively on price point.

Just ensure the bid still enables adequate delivery quality and avoids looking drastically underpriced. Seek insights into client value perceptions and price norms for the industry and type of work to orient acceptable bands.

Mitigating Pricing Risks

On fixed-price engagements, restrict promises to capabilities clearly achievable at the bid cost to avoid massive losses from misalignments with client expectations. Build in modest contingency buffers without inflating price.

Consider highlighting major cost assumptions as exclusions – for example around project durations, inflation, interest rates, exchange rates, tax regimes etc. Especially emphasize on multi-year engagements.

Propose progress payment milestones aligned to completion of key deliverables and guard against risks like late client payments through appropriate contract terms.

For overseas contracts, address unique considerations impacting local costs like applicable currencies, duties, taxes etc. Emphasize contractual mechanisms to recognize substantial inflation and currency volatility risks.

Individual Contractor Rates

Individual contractors should resist aggressive bargain pricing in their RFP responses simply to win work. This often reflects inadequate understanding of prevailing market rates. The urge to low-ball pricing frequently backfires longer-term once engaged if clients resist later increasing rates bid initially.

Instead, price with confidence at levels that reflect the true value you offer. Clients valuing top-tier work recognize pricing mismatches with average quality and pay fair rates for distinctive skills. Selling yourself short may win deals temporarily but stunts longer-term earnings growth.

Beware unscrupulous clients promising future work to get good work cheap initially but never intending repeat engagements. Cash flows now matter more than theoretical future revenue without guarantees.

Pricing done right directly enables bid success and solid project delivery. Being attentive to all cost considerations, structuring pricing thoughtfully based on work realities, and mitigating major financial risks allows for combinations of competitiveness with adequate profitability. This balancing act cements foundations for enduring client relationships built on trust and fair value exchange.

Chapter Twelve

How Clients
Evaluate Proposals

Winning a contract bid comes down to submitting a proposal that convinces the client your solution is the right fit for them. To make that case, sales teams must understand how clients assess and compare submissions to ensure their proposal stands out in the scoring. This process brings objectivity through predefined criteria but isn't always straightforward.

By learning typical evaluation methods, structures, and weighting systems, sellers can tailor proposals to align with client priorities. We'll walk through common practices, keys to strong evaluations, and strategies to overcome common pitfalls. The goal is simple: Submit proposals that showcase your value and meet client needs.

Scoring Schemes and Evaluation Matrices

Many clients, especially in the public sector, use numerical scoring schemes to rate proposals against weighted criteria. Standardized matrices facilitate apples-to-apples comparisons between bidders.

Scoring ensures traceability and transparency while enabling clients to quantify subjective factors like proposed methods or team qualifications. Evaluators score each vendor on a scale for each criterion, often from 0-3 or 0-5. They may also include comments on strengths and weaknesses.

Overall scores derive from multiplying section ratings by assigned weights. The bid with the highest total score wins the contract. Understanding the scoring approach thus helps teams emphasize critical areas in their proposals.

Weightings: Balancing Price and Quality

Bid evaluations balance scores on technical aspects ("quality") like personnel, governance, past performance and vision with cost factors ("price"). Higher quality contracts see up to an 80:20 quality-to-price ratio. More commoditized contracts use a 30:70 ratio weighted towards cheaper pricing.

Themix aims to assess best value for the money based on the work required rather than automatically selecting the lowest bid. Teams should determine the client's implied weights from the bid request content, submission instructions and scoring scheme and apportion proposal detail accordingly even if not explicitly stated.

Addressing Variations and Anomalies

Some bids allow variant solutions as long as they follow outlined procedures for fair comparisons, detailed in solicitation documents. Evaluators must also address abnormally low bids rather than rejecting them outright, asking the vendor to account for the price through extremely competitive approaches.

This aims to prevent discarding innovative, cost-effective proposals. However, bids can still get dismissed as unreliable after reconsidering the explanation. Due diligence confirming realistic pricing is key regardless of strategy.

Tiered Evaluations

Large, financially impactful agreements sometimes necessitate multi-phase bid assessments for prudent contractor selection. One approach scores all initial submissions based on technical capabilities and costs to shortlist the most competitive options. Shortlisted suppliers then refine proposals for an in-depth reevaluation. Commercial discussions may commence at this stage with only the final potential partners.

Alternately, an initial review examines a small bid excerpt to establish an access standard. Only responses clearing hurdles continue to full scoring. However, truncated excerpts risk discounting otherwise-qualified vendors due too little initial information. Suppliers mitigate this by front-loading key strengths across the entire submission from the start.

Multi-stage processes help discern top candidates when significance demands thorough vetting. But truncated initial reviews preclude top suppliers unless responses comprehensively address needs from the outset despite excerpted evaluations. Comprehensive proposals optimized for any evaluation format maximize opportunities in extensive contract competitions.

Presentations and Interviews

Some clients supplement scoring with opportunities for suppliers to directly supplement their written bids, such as interviews, product demonstrations or formal presentations. These sessions give bidders a chance to further showcase their capabilities, provide additional details and answer evaluators' questions in real-time. Supplier teams should prepare extensively for such engagements as their performance during these evaluations can help tip close scores in their favor.

Being able to confidently discuss technical aspects, relationship experience and solution specifics in person allows suppliers to substantiate their qualifications and differentiate themselves from competitors when evaluator decision-making is finely balanced. Direct interaction is a valuable way for suppliers to strengthen an already strong written case or boost a proposal's competitive standing through polished, persuasive dialogue.

Independent Review

To ensure their selection of the top contractor yields maximal advantage, some clients elect to conduct an independent review of assessments before rendering a final decision. They may engage a third-party expert to examine the evaluation process and results, checking that scoring was comprehensive and impartial. This validation also aims to affirm the recommended winning bidder most accurately represents the best balance of technical strength, cost-benefit and strategic complementarity.

Suppliers would be wise to recognize clients' drive for supplementary reassurance their selection will optimize value received. As such, proposals should take scrupulous care to substantiate pricing as fair, capabilities as exceptional and the overall fit as ideal in order to withstand the scrutiny of an added review for clients seeking rock-solid confidence in their ultimate choice of partners.

Key Takeaways

The bid process certainly incorporates some inherent complexity. However, sales teams can absolutely use these insights to improve their proposals. Remember these best practices:

- Learn the evaluation criteria, structure and weights to play to client priorities

- Balance quality and cost factors appropriately for the work

- Account for pricing anomalies transparently

- Treat tiered assessments as comprehensive opportunities

- Excel at presentations to augment paper bids

- Confirm overall value beyond just scores

Staying abreast of prevalent evaluation practices better positions your solution to come out on top during bid reviews. Sellers who understand these critical methods give clients every reason to select their proposal as the right strategic fit.

Proposal evaluations represent complex, multifaceted processes but don't need to intimidate sales teams. By breaking down scoring schemas, weighting ratios, variation procedures and supplemental evaluations, vendors can deliberately showcase their value against predefined expectations. It comes down to alignment.

When your proposal clearly communicates how your solution nails the client's technical and pricing needs at each step, whether through written content, interviews or presentations, you make their decision easy. Use this guide to optimize future bids for your best shot at winning that next big contract. What questions do you have on shaping better proposals?

Anticipating Client Questions

Winning a contract bid is about convincing clients your solution perfectly fits their needs. To make that case, proposals must provide credible answers to the questions evaluators will ask when assessing submissions.

While criteria differ across solicitations, most RFPs ultimately seek the same core information on ability to deliver. Understanding these common concerns allows vendors to proactively address client priorities throughout proposals even if not explicitly required. Anticipating and answering these evaluator concerns directly and transparently provides a strategic advantage.

Demonstrating Credibility and Experience

RFP clients want assurance that a vendor can achieve the desired outcomes based on relevant expertise. Evaluators will probe proposal claims on performance and competencies through these key questions:

- Have contractors successfully delivered comparable work before? Do client references and specifics back up stated achievements?

- Does the experience claimed come from the actual proposed project team?

- For previous engagements with this client, did contractors exhibit strong commitment to goals and responsibilities?

- Are necessary operational infrastructure and facilities readily available to facilitate delivery?

- Is the vendor officially certified or accredited in the work required?

By preemptively confirming capabilities, vendors reassure clients their project rests in qualified hands.

Validating Team Qualifications

Beyond general contractor credibility, evaluators focus heavily on whether assigned personnel carry the specific skills needed to succeed. Expect questions on:

- Do resumes demonstrate competencies and expertise at appropriate levels?

- Are roles and responsibilities clear based on background?

- What is the availability and time commitment of key staff?

- Are team members proven fully qualified employees of the vendor?

Detailing individual team members' fit for purpose eases doubts on ability to handle the client's project.

Evaluating Approach and Methodology

Aligned with needing proof of expertise, RFP clients require evidence that contractors understand objectives and have plotted an effective work plan using sound methods. Hence questions like:

- Does the proposal reflect project awareness and key priorities?

- Is the approach likely to achieve the client's goals?

- Is planning sufficiently detailed at this stage?

- Are specific techniques well-suited to the work?

- What risks or difficulties could arise, and how will the vendor mitigate them?

- Are timelines realistic while ensuring quality?

- Are deliverables and outcomes clear?

- Is the proposal tailored to client needs versus generic?

Thoroughly explaining how the work will get done provides confidence in a successful partnership.

Pricing Value and Viability

Of course proposal reviewers also gauge whether pricing aligns with budgets and represents a compelling value. Hence final confirmations around:

- Are costs within budget limitations?

- Does the total fee match the scope/quality level promised?

- Is pricing consistent and accurate throughout?

- Are expenses realistic or suggest wasted effort?

- If low, is it viably supportive of delivery while avoiding risk?

Providing transparent, competitive pricing helps seal the deal.

While RFPs have distinct focuses, nearly all include or imply these universal questions that shape evaluator decisions. Anticipating and directly addressing client concerns on credibility, personnel, approach, and costs therefore allows vendors to proactively prove their solution's advantage.

Keys to Winning Presentations

The substance of a bid - its proposed solution, expertise, and pricing - is undoubtedly most critical. However, how responses get presented also sways client perspectives. Evaluators draw conscious and unconscious impressions of quality, commitment and fit from the bid's writing, structure and usability.

Vendors who overlook proposal presentation open themselves to losing edge over competitors. This article explores best practices in crafting bids for impact beyond just good content. We'll cover writing style, document design, responsiveness and adding value. Applying these principles demonstrates attention to detail that inspires client confidence.

Cultivating Quality Writing

With complex evaluations, clients appreciate clear communication that avoids overcomplicating points. Proposals written in plain language with good flow earn higher marks for quality. Sellers should:

- Employ simple words and sentences for comprehension

- Structure logically to connect concepts

- Back claims with specifics

- Proofread carefully to prevent confusion

Bids with errors or opaque text undermine professionalism. Review processes ensuring coherence, precision and sound grammar characterize credible partners.

Structuring Documents for Ease of Use

Well-organized proposals also aid evaluations by making desired information readily accessible as reviewers navigate submissions. Effective tips include:

- Present in the sequence requested by the RFP

- Mirror formatting outlined in solicitation guidelines

- Use concise formatting as directed by clients

- Employ consistent terminology and vocabulary per RFPs

- Provide helpful visual guides like tables of contents

Meeting page limit requirements also matters as overflow content often goes ignored. Bottom line - making key messages easy to find speeds decision-making.

Responding Strategically

The best proposals not only check boxes on RFP requirements but add value through keen problem-solving. This entails:

- Directly addressing client priorities and advised discussion topics

- Exhibiting understanding of objectives and challenges

- Offering innovative ideas or distinct positioning verses competitors

- Moving past generic to showcase unique fit

Savvy teams shape responses around evaluator insights versus presenting de-contextualized capabilities. Added-value distinguishes winning solutions.

When responding to RFPs, suppliers would be wise to recognize that presentation complements substance in evaluators' assessments. Targeted, consultative proposals communicate most professionally when focused outwardly on the client's needs and perspectives, rather than inwardly on the supplier's own interests. Quality bids appear attentive to the client experience by anticipating evaluator viewpoints at each stage of review. Proper formatting, consistent branding and well-structured language showcase suppliers as thoughtful partners dedicated to clients.

Substance delievered in presentations gains credibility enhanced by appearance of expert guidance tailored to the client situation above all else. Those who lose themselves in details forget that evaluation is a relationship, not just an administrative process - outward focused communication strengthens the case for selection more than inward facts alone.

Above all, maintaining the evaluator mindset helps to improve RFP responses by design.

Chapter Thirteen

Learning From Successes and Failures

I n the competitive RFP process, every result provides an opportunity for growth. Vendors who consistently win contracts continue honing strategy based on evaluator feedback. Those less successful must diagnose shortcomings through losses to strengthen future positioning.

Bidding teams overly focused on each decision's immediate sales impact risk stagnating strategically long-term. By contrast, teams leveraging both positive and negative outcomes build capability and credibility over time. This article spotlights best practices for learning from client assessments regardless of bid results.

Requesting Constructive Criticism

Unsuccessful vendors deserve transparent explanations when an RFP loss seems opaque. Most government clients must provide scoring data and high-level perception summaries if requested. Others might offer optional debriefing sessions.

If reviewers provide only vague, legalistic responses, persist politely in extracting more tactical insights on precise deficiencies. Even limited, additional feedback exposes potential improvement areas that you can work on. Ideally, clients will share frank, specific critiques of losing proposals like:

- Perceived advantage of winning bid

- Shortcomings of credentials/experience

- Issues with approach or writing quality

- Pricing/value competitiveness

- Interview/presentation performance

Any clarification enables fact-based diagnosis versus guesswork.

Analyzing Holistically

Armed with client clarity, vendors avoidance three analysis pitfalls:

First, don't rationalize losses as inevitable due to obscure external factors. Evaluation transparency confirms whether clear internal issues undermined competitiveness.

Second, don't focus solely on price contrast explanations without considering technical merits more holistically.

Finally, don't overextrapolate isolated client feedback as revelation of major strategic gaps without reconcilement against overall market success.

The right mindset artfully synthesizes all available inputs into targeted growth opportunities without getting distracted by unrealistic inferences.

Constructing Improvement Plans

Loss diagnosis informs better bids through documented improvement initiatives across:

- Content: Enhance solution scoping, commercials, writing, positioning

- Process: Upgrade methodology, review procedures, pricing models

- Skills: Shore up qualifications shortfalls with training, new hires

- Relationships: Address engagement gaps through better communication

- Resources: Bolster infrastructure deficiencies

- Mindsets: Rightsize confidence levels

This blend of tactical and cultural actions leads to sustained excellence.

Maintaining Quality Focus

To consistently sharpen competitive proposals requires establishing learning as core to team processes beyond moments of triumph. Self-critique, transparency with client insights, and capability expansion must become routine habits independent of present achievements. Leaders foster growth by exemplifying openness to feedback, investment in growing strengths, and dedicating resources to talents' mastery. Accumulated understanding in time yields market advantages those refusing introspection cannot attain.

Ultimately, groups rejecting complacency attain the deepest insider view. What might your next shortfall unveil needing address, or victory strengthen warranting preservation? Sustained gains stem from objective reflection on experiences – does your organization leverage each proposal's lessons to collectively advance your edge? Regular considerations on performance drivers and constraints keepCapabilities stretching farther than competitors anchored in past routines. Continual refining of strengths and remedies for weaknesses prepares teams for evolving demands better than intermittent flashes of brilliance.